Unless a love affair is very conscious, it is going to create great anguish, great trouble.

All lovers are in trouble.

The trouble is not personal; it is in the very nature of things. They would not have been attracted to each other... they call it falling in love. They cannot give any reason why they have such a tremendous pull towards each other. They are not even conscious of the underlying causes; hence a strange thing happens: the happiest lovers are those who never meet.

Once they meet, the same opposition that created the attraction becomes a conflict. On each small point, their attitudes are different, their approaches are different. Although they speak the same language, they cannot understand each other.

If both partners are conscious of the fact that it is a meeting of opposites, that there is no need to make it a conflict, then it is a great opportunity to understand the totally opposite point of view and absorb it. Then the life of a man and woman together can become a beautiful harmony. Otherwise, it is continuous fight.

There are holidays. One cannot continue to fight twenty-four hours a day; one needs a little rest too – a rest to get ready for a new fight.

But it is one of the strangest phenomena that for thousands of years men and women have been living together, yet they are strangers. They go on giving birth to children, but still they remain strangers. The feminine approach and the masculine approach are so opposed to each other that unless a conscious effort is made, unless it becomes your meditation, there is no hope of having a peaceful life.

It is one of my deep concerns: how to make love and mediation so involved in each other that each love affair automatically becomes a partnership in meditation—and each meditation makes you so conscious that you need not fall in love, you can rise in love. You can find a friend consciously, deliberately.

OSHO

RISING IN LOVE...

FUSION BOOKS

Coordination: Swami Amano Surdham
Editing: Ma Deva Sarito, Mahasattva Ma Anand Savita

ISBN : 81-8419-260-6

Published by
FUSION BOOKS
X-30, Okhla Industrial Area,
Phase - II, New Delhi - 110020
Ph.: 41611861, Fax: 41611866
E-mail: sales@diamondpublication.com
Website: www.dpb.in

Edition : 2007

Printed by
Adarsh Printers, Navin Shahdara, Delhi-110032

Collection of six discourses (no. 13 to 18) from original book
Beyond Enlightenment

© **Copyright: Osho International Foundation**
All rights reserved.

No part of this book may be reproduced or transmitted in any form or by any means electronic
or mechanical including photocopying or recording or by any information storage and retrieval
system without permission in writing from **Osho International Foundation**.

Contents

OSHO

is another name for celebration, another expression for
benediction. He offers hope and confidence, love and
compassion, being and awareness to the human race
beleaguered by death and destruction, pain and suffering.
He is an invitation to experiencing a new rhythm in life,
a new dance, a new thrill in one's life.
To miss Him is to miss
the greatest blessing.

OSHO

Never born
Never died
Only visited this planet earth from
December 11, 1931 to January 19, 1990

These discourses are His spontaneous responses to live
audience, are of eternal significance, and
concern one and all.

1

THE ONLY HOLY APPROACH

Beloved Osho,

When I close my eyes, I feel such an enormous presence, such a vast isness, such a beatitude. But it is a fullness, not an emptiness.

Could You please say something about the difference between this fullness, and the emptiness or nothingness which You are speaking of?

Maitri, the fullness that you are experiencing and the nothingness that I have been speaking about are just two names for the same thing seen from two different perspectives.

If you look at it from the world of miseries, anxieties, darkness and death, it is nothingness – because all these things are absent. Your whole so-called world and its experiences are no more in it.

But if you look at what is left, or at what is revealed because of the absence of misery and darkness, then you are full of blissfulness, full of light, of enormous presence and beatitude, a great benediction. It is fullness.

It is empty of the world and full of God, it is empty of all your falsities and full of your essential reality.

Those two words are not contradictory; they are indicating the same experience from two different perspectives.

It is significant to understand that there is only one person, Gautam Buddha, who has used nothingness, emptiness, for the ultimate experience. All other mystics of the world have used fullness, wholeness, as the expression, the indication of the ultimate experience.

Why did Gautam Buddha have to choose a negative term?

It is significant to understand – for your own spiritual growth, not for any philosophical reasons. I do not speak for philosophical reasons. I speak only when I see there is some existential relevance.

The idea of fullness, the idea of God, the idea of perfection, the idea of the absolute, the ultimate – all are positive terms. And Gautam Buddha was amazed to see the cunningness of human mind.

The innocent mystics have simply used the positive words because that was their experience. Why bother about the misery which is no more? Why not say something about that which is now? The innocent mystics have spoken out of their isness. But throughout the centuries the cunning minds of people around the world have taken advantage of it.

To the cunning mind, the idea of fullness and the positive terms indicating it became an ego trip: "*I* have to become God. *I* have to attain the absolute, the *brahma; I* have to achieve the ultimate liberation." The *I* became the center of all our assertions.

And the trouble is that you cannot make the ultimate experience a goal for the ego.

Ego is the barrier; it cannot become the bridge.

So all the positive terms have been misused. Rather than destroying the ego, they have become decorations for the ego. God has become a goal, you have to achieve the goal. *You* become greater than God.

Remember, the goal cannot be greater than you. The achieved cannot be greater than the achiever. It is a very simple fact to understand.

And all the religions have fallen because of this simple innocence of the mystics.

Gautam Buddha was the most cultured and the most educated, the most sophisticated person ever to become a mystic. There is no comparison in the whole of history. He could see where the innocent mystics had unknowingly given chances for cunning minds to take advantage. He decided not to use any positive term for the ultimate goal, to destroy your ego and any possibility of your ego taking any advantage.

He called the ultimate, nothingness, emptiness, *shunyata,* zero. Now, how can the ego make zero the goal? God can be made the goal, but not zero.

Who wants to become zero? – that is the fear. Everybody is avoiding all possibilities of becoming zero, and Buddha made it an expression for the ultimate.

His word is *nirvana*.

He chose a tremendously beautiful word, but he shocked all the thinkers and philosophers by choosing the word *'nirvana'* as the most significant expression for the ultimate experience.

Nirvana means blowing out the candle.

The other mystics have said that you are filled with enormous light, as if thousands of suns together have suddenly risen inside you, as if the whole sky full of stars has descended within your heart.

These ideas appeal to the ego.

The ego would like to have all the stars, if not inside the chest then at least hanging on the coat outside the chest. "Enormous light" ... the ego is very willing.

To cut the very roots, Buddha says the experience is as if you were to blow out a candle. There was a small flame on the candle giving a small light – even that is gone, and you are surrounded with absolute darkness, abysmal darkness.

People used to come to ask him, "If you go on teaching such things, nobody is going to follow you. Who wants darkness, enormous darkness? You are crazy. You say that the ultimate experience is ultimate death. People want eternal life, and you are talking about ultimate death."

But he was a very consistent man, and you can see that for forty-two years he hammered on the genius of the East without ever compromising with the ego.

He also knows that what he is calling darkness is too much light; that's why it looks like darkness. If one thousand suns rise in you, what do you think? – that you will feel enormous light? You will feel immense darkness, it will be too dazzling. Just look at *one* sun for a few seconds – and you will feel your eyes are going blind. If one thousand suns are within you, inside the mind, the experience will be of darkness, not of light.

It will take a long time for you to get accustomed, for your eyes to become strong enough to see – slowly, slowly – darkness turning into light, death turning into life, emptiness turning into fullness.

But he never talked about those things. He never said that darkness would ever turn into light.

And he never said that death would become a resurrection at some later point, because he knows how cunning your ego is. If that is said, the ego will say, "Then there is no problem. Our aim remains the same; it is just that we will have to pass through a little dark night of the soul. But finally, we will have enormous light, thousands of suns."

Gautam Buddha had to deny that God existed – not that he was against God, a man like Gautam Buddha cannot be against God. And if Gautam Buddha is against God, then it is of no use for anybody to be in favor of God. His decision is decisive for the whole of humanity, he represents our very soul. But he was not against God. He was against your ego, and he was constantly careful not to give your ego any support to remain. If God can become a support, then there is no God.

One thing becomes very clear: although he used, for the first time, all negative terms, yet the man must have had tremendous charismatic qualities. He influenced millions of people.

His philosophy is such that anyone listening to him would freak out. What is the point of all the meditations and all the austerities, renouncing the world, eating one time a day ... and ultimately you achieve nothingness, you become zero! We are already better – we may be miserable zeros, but we *are* at least.

Certainly, when you are *completely* a zero there cannot be any misery; zeros are not known to be miserable – but what is the gain?

But he convinced people not through his philosophy, but through his individuality, through his presence. He gave people the experience itself, so that they could understand: it is emptiness as far as the world is concerned, it is emptiness for the ego. And it is fullness for the being.

There are many reasons for the disappearance of Buddha's thought from India, but this is one of the most significant. All other Indian mystics, philosophers, and seers have used positive terms.

And for centuries before Buddha, the whole of India was accustomed to thinking only in the positive; the negative was something unheard of. Under the influence of Gautam Buddha they followed him, but when he died his following started disappearing – because the following was not intellectually convinced; it was convinced because of his presence.

Because of the eyes of Gautam Buddha they could see: "This man – if he is living in nothingness then there is no fear, we would love to be nothing. If this is where zeroness leads, if by being nothing such lotuses bloom in the eyes and such grace flows, then we are ready to go with this man. The man has a magic."

But his philosophy alone will not convince you, because it has no appeal for the ego.

And Buddhism survived in China, in Ceylon (Sri Lanka), in Burma, in Japan, in Korea, in Indochina, in Indonesia – in the whole of Asia except India – because the Buddhists who reached there dropped negative terms. They started speaking in positive terms. Then the ultimate, the absolute, the perfect – the old terms returned. This was the compromise.

So as far as I am concerned, Buddhism died with Gautam Buddha. Whatever exists now as Buddhism has nothing to do with Buddha because it has dropped his basic contribution, and that was his negative approach.

I am aware of both traditions. I am certainly in a better position than Gautam Buddha was. Gautam Buddha was aware of only one thing – that the ego can use the positive. And it is his great contribution, his courageous contribution, that he dropped the positive and insisted on the negative, emphasized the negative – knowing perfectly well that people were not going to follow this because it had no appeal for the ego.

To me, now both traditions are available. I know what happened to the positive – the ego exploited it. I know what happened to the negative. After the death of Gautam Buddha, the disciples had to compromise, compromise with the same thing which Gautam Buddha was revolting against.

So I am trying to explain to you both approaches together – emptiness as far as the world is concerned and fullness, wholeness as far as the inner experience is concerned. And this is a total approach, it takes note of both: that which has to be left behind, and that which is to be gained.

I call my approach the only holy approach.

All other approaches up to now have been half-half. Mahavira, Shankara, Moses, Mohammed, all used the positive. Gautam Buddha used the negative. I use both, and I don't see any contradiction.

If you understand me clearly, then you can enjoy the beauty of both viewpoints, and you need not be exploited by your ego or be afraid of death and darkness and nothingness.

Maitri, they are not two things. It is almost as if I were to put a glass of water in front of you, half full and half empty, and ask you whether the glass is empty or full. Either answer would be wrong, because the glass is both half full and half empty. From one side it is empty, from another side it is full.

Half of your life is part of the mundane world, the other half is part of the sacred. And it is unfortunate, but there is no other way – we have to use the same language for both the mundane and the sacred.

So one has to be very alert. To choose the mundane will be missing; if you think of the mundane, you will find the sacred life empty. If you think of the sacred, you will find it overflowingly full.

Beloved Osho

As You were talking about Indian and Western sannyasins, *I felt what You were saying was true — sometimes the Indians are too much of the heart. It is hard to say no to them, yet you cannot say yes to their expectations and theories. They are deaf. Will You please explain why this is so?*

The question has many parts.

The first part, that the Indians are sometimes too much of the heart ... that statement is wrong. One can never be too much of the heart; that is existentially impossible.

The heart and its qualities are such that you can always have more of them. And there is no limit — not even the sky is the limit.

But I understand your problem. You are saying that you are finding it difficult in certain moments, the people of the East are too much loving; you cannot say no to them and you cannot say yes either.

I am reminded of when I came to Bombay for the first time, I was invited for lunch ... I was new, and the people who had invited me here were new. None of us knew each other.

The man had come to Bombay just two or three days before. He is one of the most beautiful men I have met in my life. Along with me, he had invited at least twenty more people. It was beautiful food, but the way they were forcing everybody to eat was just unimaginable.

They were three brothers; two of the brothers would hold the person, and the third one would force him – "One *laddu* more."

And the person would be trying to say, "I will die! Leave me!"

They would say, "Just one..." And this was something unending.

Even the women of the house were helping. People were trying to run out of the room and the women were standing in the doorway.

I asked the man, "Your love is good, and your sweets are good, but there is a limit. That man is saying he will die – and you are not concerned about his death, you are concerned about forcing more food on him."

What he said to me I have not forgotten. He said, "If we don't do this, my father's soul will be very unhappy."

I said, "My God! Is your father's soul also present here?"

He said, "No, that is not the question. This is our heritage. In my father's day, this was the routine: unless the guest starts fighting and beating you, don't leave him alone. Things have to come to that end."

I said, "Listen, don't do this thing to me – because I cannot beat you, and neither do I want to fight."

They said, "But our father's soul...."

I said, "You are idiots! Your father's soul must have been born **again** by now. When did your father die?"

They said, "It must be twenty years."

I said, "He must be in a college somewhere studying. Forget about him, he has nothing to do with it."

He said, "If you say so.... But we will feel very guilty."

I said, "If you force anything on me, I am not going to come to Bombay again."

With tears in his eyes, he took hold of my legs. He said, "That's perfectly good. I will not force you. Just one *laddu*, no fight, but please continue to come. And promise me that at least whenever you come ... one lunch at my house, and we will never force you. Just have one more *laddu*.".

I said, "But you *are* forcing me! This is another strategy – tears, holding my leg; it is no different from holding my neck. It is even worse, because I feel that although it will create trouble for me – you have forced so many sweets on me – looking at your tears...."

He said, "What can I do? Just thinking of my father's soul...."

I said, "Drop your father's soul! Do you promise me that if I take this *laddu* you will not ask anything?"

He said, "I absolutely promise."

But I was not aware of the strategy. It was one brother's promise – they were three brothers, with three wives....

I said, "My God, it seems soon my soul is going to meet your father's soul! If you have any message, I will deliver it to him. And I will never come again."

And they were all sitting on the floor, holding my leg – "You have to come."

Love is one thing ... this is not love.

Because love would take care of me, see that I don't fall sick. They are taking care of their father's soul, they are not concerned with me.

So I can understand your question, that sometimes their love is too much, their heart is too much. You cannot say no and you cannot say yes either.

But you have to be very clear with the people in the East. Accept their love, be grateful for their love, but when it goes against your reason, "no" is not something that cannot be said. It is not necessarily against love. You are simply protecting yourself, and you have the right to protect yourself. If you cannot say yes, don't say yes.

And remember: what they are doing is not love, but some formality, some tradition, some convention. This is not part of love. They are fulfilling their own traditional, conventional, orthodox views.

If it were love then food would not be forced; then the guest would be served and allowed to eat whatever he feels like eating, and however much he wants to eat. Love will give that freedom.

It is not heart. The dividing line is very fine – that's why you cannot understand how to say no. He is so loving that it seems better to suffer a little, but not to say no. But this is not his love.

Love never enforces anything on anyone.

Love never tries to dominate, to dictate.

You call this love? – two persons are holding onto the man's hands and the third person is forcing a *laddu* into his mouth, and the man is saying, "I will die! What are you doing? If you had told me that this was going to happen I would have never come."

But they have a certain idea. It has been happening in their family for centuries – unless a guest starts beating you, you are not a host, not worth the name. A strange idea!

You have to say no. And if they need beating, then it is better that before they force the food, you start beating them. If that is the only thing that will stop them and satisfy them and their father's soul, then beat them before they make you sick.

Be alert, and understand clearly the idea of love. It is non-interfering. It is non-enforcing – about *anything*.

Love is authentic only when it gives you freedom.

I am reminded of a strange Eastern story that will show you what love is.

A man is in great love with a woman. The woman says, "I am ready to marry you, but there is one condition."

If the man had been aware of a simple fact, that love never makes conditions, he would have said goodbye to the woman at that very point. But he was mad, really blindly in love. He was ready to do anything. He said, "Any condition, and I am ready to do it."

The woman said, "My condition is difficult."

The man said, "Whatever the condition is, don't be worried. You just say it."

The woman said, "Go home and kill your mother. Bring her heart on a plate and present it to me. Only on this condition will I marry you, because only this will give me proof that you really love me."

Blind lovers can do anything. They *are*, not only in this story but all over the world.

He went home, he killed his mother, and he put her heart on a plate ... he rushed. He was in such a hurry to reach the woman that he stumbled on the road and fell. The plate broke and the heart was all over the street in small pieces.

And a voice came from those pieces: "My son, are you hurt? I am sorry, but it wasn't my fault. Try to gather the pieces; go home and get another plate, and go to your sweetheart."

Listening to this, it was as if he suddenly awoke from a dream. What was he doing? What had he done? And his mother has not still complained, is not even angry. On the contrary, she had inquired, "Are you hurt? – because you've fallen on the ground. I have always been telling you to go slowly, but you never listen to me. Now collect all the pieces and go back home."

He collected the pieces, went home, and forgot all about that woman.

The woman waited and waited. One day passed, another day passed. She said, "What happened?" She went to the man's house, found that he had killed his mother. She said, "What happened then? Where is the heart?"

It was on a plate, in fragments.

He said, "This is the heart, but something happened on the road that made me turn back. I knew for the first time what love means. I am grateful to you; otherwise I would have never understood that my mother was so much concerned about my welfare. And I cannot forgive myself, that I killed the woman with my own hands. As for you, who asked such a condition...!"

Love makes no conditions.

Love gives you freedom to be yourself, helps you to be yourself. Even if it goes against his own interest, still, a loving person will suffer himself rather than make the loved one suffer.

Another ancient story....

A woman loved her husband, but the husband never paid any attention to her. He was in love with a prostitute, knowing perfectly well that prostitutes don't love – because there were many other customers. He was *only* a customer, not a lover. And in his life he had seen that the day the customer's money is finished, the prostitute's door is closed for that man.

He had destroyed his health, he had destroyed his money, now he was dying. Just as he was dying, his wife asked him, "If you have any last wish so that you can die contented...."

He said, "Yes, I have a wish, but I am ashamed to say it to you."

She said, "Don't be ashamed. This is not the time to be ashamed. I love you as you are – there is no question of feeling ashamed."

He said, "My only wish is to see the prostitute just once more before I die."

The woman said, "There is no problem:"

He had lost all the money, there was no money in the house. She had to carry the dying man on her shoulders to the prostitute's house. She knocked on the door.

The prostitute opened the door and could not believe it. She said, "Am I hallucinating? Is this real? You are the wife of the man...."

The wife said, "Yes, I am the wife and also the lover of the man."

The prostitute said, "Then why have you brought him here? He destroyed your life, he spent all your money and he was mad after me. And to me, once the money is finished, all relationship is finished. He was only a customer. This is a marketplace and he knows it. You are a strange woman!"

She said, "But this was his dying wish. He wanted to see you, and I love him so much that I could not say no. In his happiness is my happiness, and if he can die contented I will feel I have fulfilled my duty, my love."

No complaint about the man, about his whole behavior. No jealousy against the woman.

Love knows no jealousy, love knows no complaint.

Love is a deep understanding.

You love someone – that does not mean that the other should love you also. It is not a contract.

Try to understand the meaning of love.

And you will not be able to understand the meaning of love by your so-called love affairs.

Strangely enough, you will understand the meaning of love by going deep into meditation, by becoming more silent, more together, more at ease. You will stare radiating a certain energy. You will become loving, and you will know the beautiful qualities of love. It knows to say yes, it also knows to say no. It is not blind.

But it has to come out of your meditation – only then does love have eyes; otherwise love *is* blind.

And unless love has eyes, it is worthless. It is going to create more and more trouble for you – because two blind persons with blind expectations are not only going to double the troubles of life, they are going to multiply the troubles of life.

So be silent and be alert. Be loving.

And you can say no with great love. No does not mean that you are unloving; yes does not mean that you are loving. Sometimes yes may mean that you are simply afraid, it is out of fear. So it is not necessarily that love means yes and you cannot say no.

Love with eyes knows when to say no, when to say yes.

Love neither interferes in anybody's life nor allows anybody else to interfere into one's own life.

Love gives individuality to others, but does not lose its own individuality.

And it is not a question of Western or Eastern – what I am saying is applicable to all. Just because you have asked the question as if the problem is because you come from the West....

It has to be understood well: it is not a question of your coming from the West; it is a problem because reason and heart are always in conflict. And the West is more rationalist, but the West has spread all over the world through its empires and through its educational systems. Now it is very difficult to find a purely Eastern man. The West has poisoned everybody.

Reason has become supreme.

So try to understand it in terms of reason and heart, not in terms of West and East. Because even in the East, for the people who are living in their reason – and all people who are cultured, educated, are living in their reason – the problem is the same.

The heart has its own language, reason has *its* own language, and they are not necessarily always in agreement. Most probably they are in disagreement, because reason thinks in a different dimension.

I am reminded of Albert Einstein and his wife, Frau Einstein. His wife was a poet. And he was just the wrong person to be married to – a mathematician, a physicist. In mathematics, one plus one is always two. In love, one plus one is always one. Languages are so different.

And Frau Einstein was a talented woman; naturally she wanted to show a few of her poems to Albert Einstein, and would have enjoyed being appreciated by the world's most famous mathematician, physicist, scientist. But she could not see any emotion moving in Albert Einstein's face, or any changes in his eyes. He listened to her poems as if he were a stone statue.

She had written a beautiful piece, talking about the beloved and comparing the face of the beloved with the moon.

At that point, Einstein said, "Enough! Stop! This is too much. You don't understand anything about the moon. Do you know its proportions? If a moon were put on a man's body as a head, your beloved would not be found again, he would be crushed to pieces. And who told you that the moon is beautiful? It is a dead rock, with no water, no greenery, no flowers, no trees, no birds. Who told you that the moon is beautiful? What do you mean by beauty?"

The wife was shocked, she could not believe that such a great scientist would talk in such a way. But he was not joking – that's how reason thinks.

Reason cannot understand poetry; it is not its way.

It is very prose.

Frau Einstein has written in her memoirs, "That was the first and the last time I ever mentioned poetry to him. It would be better to talk to a rock; perhaps the rock might respond better than this man."

The question is not of East and West. The question is between the heart and the reason.

In the East, the heart has been predominant, but it has created a problem which nobody has discussed.

I have been looking through ancient scriptures, literature, commentaries – has anybody ever thought about this problem or not?– because it is so significant it cannot be ignored. Because the East is leaning too much towards the heart, it has not developed rationality to its fullest – but still it goes on talking about theories, reincarnation, heaven and hell. If you were to say that these are mythological, there would be no problem, but people insist that these are rational hypotheses.

And your question is relevant: it becomes so difficult to talk with the Eastern person because he goes on talking about theories which look absurd, stupid, illogical. But to him they seem absolutely valid because he has never been trained in reason. His validity is of the heart.

I will give you a few examples so you can understand.

Jainas say that once a snake bit Mahavira on his foot, and instead of blood coming out, milk came out. Now, if you say it is a myth, a parable, a poetry, there is no problem....

The first time I spoke in Bombay, one Jaina monk, Chitrabhanu, had spoken ahead of me. And he mentioned this fact, and gave the reason why milk came out: because Mahavira is so full of love that even when a snake bites him, it is because of his love and compassion that milk comes out – just a little breakfast for the snake. No anger, no violence...

And for twenty-five centuries Jainas have been writing in their books that this is factual.

I was to speak after Chitrabhanu.

I said, "If it is factual then many things have to be explained: it means that Mahavira's body was filled with milk instead of blood. And the snakebite happened when he was near about fifty, so for fifty years ... all the milk would have certainly turned into curd. And he used to walk naked, on foot ... in fifty years' time, the curd would have turned into butter! And in such heat, in such a hot country, butter is going to become *ghee*."

So if *ghee* had come out of his foot instead of blood, there would be some rationality to it – but milk? And this is so stupid, that a man is full of curd ... he would stink of curd! Fifty years filled with curd and butter and ghee – just think of that poor man. In the hot season, he wouldn't perspire, he would start flowing with ghee!

So I said, "This is nonsense. The only possibility is: milk comes out of a woman's body, and she has a certain mechanism in her breast to transform the blood into milk. A rational mind could accept it, that Mahavira had the same mechanism in his feet. His feet were nothing but breasts. And strangely... was he expecting that the snake was going to bite him on the foot? Most probably, he had breasts all over, so that wherever the snake bit, milk would come out."

And even a woman's breast will not give milk unless she has given birth to a child. So I said, "This goes on and on into difficulties. It is better to simply accept that this is poetry. Don't make it history. Don't try to theorize it, don't try to make it scientific. Simply say that it is a poetic way of saying that he was so loving ... how to say it in poetry? So we have expressed it by saying that milk came out, just as the milk comes out of the mother's breast, in love."

Milk has a certain association with love, because the child receives the milk and love from the same breast – that is his first experience in the world. And that's why humanity is so obsessed with the breast. Painters go on painting breasts and breasts, sculptors go on making breasts and breasts.

Poets, novelists, all kinds of creative people are obsessed only with one object, and that is the woman's breast. The reason is clear: it is the child's first experience of love, of warmth, of the human body, of the other, of the world. It contains so much. So just to give expression to a feeling of love and warmth, milk has been used as a symbol.

But no Jaina is going to agree with me, because then the miracle is lost. Poetry is not a miracle. The miracle is in the historicity of the fact.

So you are right in questioning how to deal with these people. They are so loving, they are so full of heart, but they go on talking about such nonsense ... esoteric, occult.

And everybody in the East knows so much that it seems that all are realized souls! Where to stop these people, and where to say no to these people?

You have to be very clear, very loving, but without any compromise. The moment you see that these people are going into fictions and creating stupid theories – and their scriptures are full of them – you have to stop them.

That is one of the misfortunes of the East, that people have forgotten completely that poetry is not history, that poetry is far more significant than history. Then theorizations, rationalizations are meaningless, and the effort to prove them as if they are scientific truths makes the whole East a laughing stock.

My own approach is very simple:

You have to be alert not to allow the heart to start overpowering your reason, just as you have to be alert that your reason does not overpower your heart. Their functions are separate. Reason should function in the world of objects, and the heart should function in the world of human consciousness. And the moment they overlap, there is going to be a certain kind of mess.

And whenever you feel it, that the man is so loving, how to say no to him? Don't be worried. It has been my whole life's difficulty – because everybody in India is so full of knowledge, and all that knowledge is simply holy cow dung, there is nothing in it.

But these people are good, this is the problem. The people are good: very generous, very loving, very helpful. Only their hearts have overrun their heads, so whatsoever they are saying ... you have to be a little alert.

And when you say no to them, they feel hurt; they think their love is rejected. So you have to be very careful and very articulate.

It is a difficult task – it was for me, because with my family, my teachers, my professors ... everywhere I was in difficulty. Because I could not see how a well-educated professor could be talking such nonsense, without even being aware at all that what he is saying is nonsense. And he is a good man, there is no doubt about his sincerity. It is simply that his reason is retarded. Only the heart has grown, and it has its beauty. But the heart is leading the reason, so they are talking all kinds of nonsense.

I had to stop them – "Wait a minute. You cannot say this rationally. Either accept it as a poetry or withdraw it."

But the result was that I was expelled from this college, from that university – and they had no reason.

The vice-chancellor said to me, "We don't have any reason to expel you, you have not done anything that demands such a punishment. But you should understand our difficulty: you are creating such trouble to so many professors that they are threatening to resign if you don't leave this university. And we cannot afford it, those are our very respected professors."

And I said, "First you should call them and ask them what the problem is, why they are so angry with me."

And the professors said, "It is not a question of being angry with you. You simply raise questions which make us feel embarrassed before the whole class. And people laugh, and we cannot answer. You are destroying the respectability we have established over thirty years, forty years – you, within half an hour, destroy the whole of it. People lose all respect for us."

And I said, "Have I ever shown any disrespect to you?"

They said, "You never show any disrespect. That is not the question, the question is that we cannot change now. Our whole lives we have lived with certain theories. And we have believed them to be scientific, we have never suspected them. Suddenly you come here, and on each point you create a question and we are at a loss."

One of the professors was a celibate, and he was continually preaching celibacy, that the only spirituality is to be celibate.

I asked him, "I have been in your home, and I see Rama there with Sita, the Hindu god Rama standing with his wife, Sita. What kind of celibacy is this fellow following? And out of this celibacy two children are born – you should throw this fellow out of your house! But you worship him, and in the university you talk about celibacy. Do you see the contradiction or not? All your *Vedic* seers were married people, all your *Upanishadic* seers were married people. You read *Shrimad Bhagavadgita* every day, and this fellow Shri Krishna had sixteen thousand wives – what kind of celibacy is this?"

Now this man took my hand and told me, "Come with me to the vice-chancellor. This is too much – now either you are going to remain in the university or I am going to remain in the university."

But I said, "I have simply asked a question. You can satisfy me by giving a satisfying answer. Or, you can say that you are greater than all these people because you are celibate and they were not. But why are you worshipping them? They should worship you."

On the way, he asked me, "Should we go to the vice-chancellor or not?"

I said, "It is up to you. Because the whole question will be discussed, and I will insist that the vice-chancellor have a look in your house. You have made a temple where Rama is standing with Sita and Krishna is standing with Rukmani – which is absolute hypocrisy; he was married to this woman Rukmani but he never lived with her. How could he manage it? Sixteen thousand wives stolen from other people's houses ... he was married to only one woman; the remaining ones were all stolen, forcibly taken. Whenever he saw a beautiful woman, his soldiers would take her – no consideration of the husband or the children or the old parents, no consideration at all. And still, the hypocrisy is that you are putting poor Rukmani next to Krishna. I will take the vice-chancellor to have a look in your house and things can be decided then and there."

I said, "There is no need for you to resign. You simply don't be celibate, get married! The problem will be solved – neither I will have to be expelled from the university nor will you have to resign. And if you feel shy, I will find a good wife for you."

He said, "You stop! Don't talk like this, you are almost persuading me. This is seduction!"

I said, "Then come on and see the vice-chancellor."

And we went, and the vice-chancellor listened, and he told me, "You are not wrong, but what can we do? As far as Indian logic is concerned, this man is the best in the whole of India. We cannot...."

I said, "You just think – this man is absolutely illogical. How can he be an expert in Indian logic? His behavior is so illogical ... a celibate worshipping married people."

But the vice-chancellor said, "You had better choose some other university. I will recommend you. I will not expel you, I will recommend you as highly as possible." But no university was ready to accept me, because my fame had reached ahead of me already – that that fellow is coming to be admitted to the university or the college.

In India it is a problem – people are not rational. Even th. pretend to be rational, their behavior is very irrational.

They will be very loving, but don't allow them to destroy your reason. The heart has to grow, reason has to become sharp – because both have to fulfill their functions in the totality of your growth.

A man with a great heart and a great intelligence, without any conflict between them, is truly a genius.

And everybody has the possibility, but everybody is either dominated by logic or dominated by the heart. Everybody is living a lopsided life.

Have you seen any advertisements for circuses? When a circus comes to a town – I have seen it in many towns – they have bicycles, with one wheel small and one wheel big. And the big wheel's center is not in the center, it is off-center.

So the man riding on the bicycle comes up, goes down, comes up, goes down – naturally he attracts everybody's attention – "What is happening?" A man suddenly comes up and goes down ... and he is a joker, wearing the joker's dress ... and the name of the circus, and the timings and the tickets and everything....

A single man will attract everybody – a simple device.

But seeing that kind of advertisement, I saw that this is the situation of almost every man.

You have two wheels, the reason and the heart.

Somebody's heart is big and their reason is small – then he goes up and down.

Somebody's reason is big and his heart is small – then he goes up and down.

Everybody is going up and down – and for whom are you advertising?

And it is not easy to sit on that bicycle, I have tried it. It is a very difficult job.

But people are living this way – unbalanced.

You need a balanced life in which reason and heart move in harmony, supporting each other, helping each other. So whenever you see that anybody – either from the East or from the West – is disturbing your harmony, stop him.

Stop him lovingly, there is no need to be rude.

But don't be silent, because to be silent is to be rude. You have allowed that man to move in a wrong way, you were not compassionate enough.

●●●

2

DON'T BE A MISSIONARY, BE A MESSAGE

Beloved Osho,

You heard my prayer and called me to You on the 8th of August. As I entered Your room, I experienced You as large ocean, an emptiness that I have never experienced before. I saw Your beautiful being, and I was immersed in that emptiness and beauty. I felt that the ocean's emptiness was flowing into me from You. After that day, new songs and melodies are coming from that emptiness of Yours, and I don't know anything.

Beloved Osho, please explain how this can happen so easily in the master's presence. Is it so simple? It doesn't feel possible for me to exist in this life without having had that meeting – is that so? I feel that such a feeling might not have otherwise happened to me for many lives. Please explain the meeting of the master and the disciple.

Ashok Bharti, the most obvious in life seems to be a the most difficult; the most simple seems to be the most complicated. The reason why it happens so, is because the mind is not interested in the obvious.

It wants the challenge of the impossible; only with the challenge of the impossible can the mind fulfill its ego. With the obvious, there is no space for the ego to grow or even to exist.

The obvious is the grave of the ego. The simple we take for granted, because it is so simple. Only the far away, the distant, catches our eye, invites us for a journey. Because of this, people have gone around the earth – people like Columbus. People have gone to the moon, people are trying to go to Mars, people are thinking to reach some day to the most distant stars.

Nobody bothers to enter into himself, and to see the most miraculous, the most mysterious, the most fundamental principle of life, the very source of life – it is so close, so obvious, so simple.

People may not find anything on the moon; they have not found anything, but they have become great historical figures.

Edmund Hillary has not found anything on Everest, but his name will remain a landmark forever.

I have always been surprised that for at least one hundred years people from all the Western countries have been coming to climb the highest peak of the Himalayas, Everest. No Indian has bothered about it; for the Indian it is so obvious.

The more difficult a thing is, the more attractive it is; the more unattainable, the more mind becomes obsessed.

I have heard, a great psychologist was visiting a madhouse. The superintendent of the madhouse was taking him on a tour, satisfying his curiosities and questions about the inmates.

He became immensely interested in one inmate; behind the bars, in his cell, he was standing naked. On the wall there was a small picture of an ordinary woman, and he was standing in a worshipful mood, tears flowing from his eyes. The psychologist asked, "What is the matter with this man?"

The superintendent said, "Don't disturb him," took him a little away, and said, "He does not like to be disturbed in his prayers, and he is praying almost the whole day."

The psychologist said, "Whose picture is that?"

The superintendent started laughing. He said, "It is nobody, it is just an ordinary woman. He was in love, but because they belonged to different castes, the father of the woman refused; he became mad and the woman became a goddess. Unattainable, one ordinary woman became a goddess. Now he worships and prays that, 'What has not happened in this life, perhaps through prayer and worship may happen in the next.'"

The psychologist said, "I have never come across such a case."

The superintendent said, "Just wait a little more."

In the next cell there was another man who was hitting his head against the wall, and two guards were holding him. The psychologists said, "What has happened to him? Why does he want to hit his head on the wall?"

The superintendent said, "He has gone mad. He wants to commit suicide, and it is such a problem to watch him continuously – he hurts himself."

"But what is the cause of his madness?"

The superintendent said, "That's why I was, telling you to just wait a little. He got married, and the marriage has been such a disaster that he is in the madhouse. He wants to commit suicide. Because sooner or later he will be sent out of the madhouse, and again be in the hands of that woman. But it is the same woman! And to avoid her, he wants to commit suicide."

The psychologist said, "My God, it is the same woman the other man is praying to get in his next life? – because he missed the train this time! And this poor fellow did not miss this time – now *he* wants to jump out of the train. He can't even wait for the station to come."

Life is not logic. Life is love.

Logic is a complicated phenomenon.

Love is simple, innocent communion.

Life is closer to music than to mathematics, because mathematics is of the mind, and life throbs in your heartbeats.

Ashok Bharti, you love me and that opens the door for all the mysteries possible.

People say love is blind because they do not know what love is.

I say unto you, only love has eyes; other than love, everything is blind.

Once your eyes of love are opened, things which you have never dreamed of start becoming realities; new songs that you had never thought yourself capable of, new poetries, with such insights that you cannot believe that you have written them.

This is the reason why all the ancient scriptures don't have the names of their authors – because the authors could not believe that they were the writers of the *Upanishads,* of the *Vedas.* They could not believe it. At the most, they have been vehicles; they were possessed. Some universal energy has taken possession of them, and what they have written has nothing to do with them. They have not signed the scriptures that they have written.

It is very difficult to find out who are the sculptors of the most beautiful ancient statues of Gautam Buddha, which have never again been paralleled.

The grand architectures of the caves of Ajanta, Ellora ... it seems almost superhuman work, and the people have not even signed their names because they never believed that they were doing it. They experienced that existence was using them as instruments, and they were blessed and grateful that they had been chosen to be instrumental. Existence has been compassionate towards them; they are enough rewarded.

Ashok Bharti is a poor man, but has a very rich heart; and to have a rich heart is the only real richness in the world. He has the potentiality of becoming a great singer, a great poet, a great composer, but he was not aware of it.

He had come just to see me; he's my old *sannyasin*. And knowing that to me, religion means celebration, he brought his *khanjhari* – just to sing a song to me; what else to bring as an offering? He was very shy in asking, "Can I sing a song in Your presence?"

I said, "This is the most beautiful present anyone could have brought to me. You can sing every day." And I have been watching him for almost one month – the depth, the significance, the meaning of his songs has been deepening. His courage is growing, he is no more hesitant, he is not worried that so many people are watching. He is not a public singer – he's just like everybody else, a bathroom singer.

It is strange – in bathrooms you will find the great singers of the world, but the moment you bring them out of the bathroom they become dumb.

Everybody is a good conversationalist. The whole world is agog with people talking to each other, but just put somebody on a pedestal, and he looks at the crowd watching him and his heart starts sinking. These are the same people he has been talking to separately, privately. But to be observed with thousands of eyes ... a fear arises that, "If something goes wrong, I will become a laughing stock before so many people."

I have been watching Ashok. The first day there was that fear. Slowly slowly, the fear has disappeared; on the contrary, a fearlessness, a strength....

And he has been creating his own songs, tremendously beautiful – not composed by the mind, but arising out of his love and out of his heart. They have a totally different beauty.

It is true, Ashok, that if you love me you will feel in my presence as if you are disappearing into a vast emptiness, or into a vast fullness.

Beyond human mind, emptiness and fullness mean the same thing.

Love makes you empty – empty of jealousy, empty of power trips, empty of anger, empty of competitiveness, empty of your ego and all its garbage.

But love also makes you full of things which are unknown to you right now; it makes you full of fragrance, full of light, full of joy.

An ancient story is, a king is getting old.... He has three sons, and all are intelligent. They are triplets, born together, so there is no question of who is the eldest; otherwise, there would have been no problem, the eldest son would have been the successor. The problem was, who out of the three is going to be the successor? They are all of the same age. In horse riding they are all of equal efficiency; in archery they are equally great. In every field it is impossible to decide who is the best of the three.

He asked his master, an old wise man living in the forest: "I am getting old, and somebody has to succeed me and take care of the kingdom. And I am in great difficulty: can you give me some idea how to choose the right person?" And the wise man gave him some advice.

The king came back, and he gave an equal amount of money to all three sons and told them – because they all had their own palaces – that, "With this money, you have to manage to fill your palaces completely. And after seven days I will come to see: whoever succeeds in filling the house totally, better than the other two, is going to succeed me as the king of the kingdom."

They were puzzled, because the money was not that great. They thought of many things, but the palaces were big – how to fill them completely?

The first prince went to the municipal corporation and asked, "From today, all the trucks that throw the garbage of the town outside the city should throw it into my palace – because with that money only this much is possible, to fill the palace completely."

He filled the palace completely. The whole neighborhood was angry; even the traffic on the road stopped – because it was stinking. But they could not do anything – he was the prince, and it was a question of a certain test. The king himself has asked.

The second prince was very much worried ... asked many people. But they said, "With such a small amount of money it is very difficult.

What your brother has done ... he has filled the house; you can do something similar. Just purchase cheap grass, fill the house." He purchased cheapest quality of grass, which even animals were not ready to eat, but still the house was not full; it was only half full.

They were both worried about what the third brother was doing, because he looked absolutely unconcerned. Six days had passed and he had not done anything. And the seventh day came, and by the evening, as the sun set, the king came with the wise old man.

It was impossible to come close to the first son's house.

The king said, "This idiot, he has really filled the house – but with garbage! It is disgusting, I am feeling sick."

But the old man said, "You had asked ... and we have to go and see. Just have a little patience. You need not stay long; just have a look to see whether he has filled the house or not." They saw it.

They went to the second son's house.... It was not better, but it was not worse either. It was rotten grass, but the house was half full.

The king was very much disappointed – so much so that he thought that it would be better not to go to the house of the third prince. Because these idiots ... what they have done is not worth seeing.

But the wise man said, "You have to go, because the decision has to be taken."

They went to the house of the third young man. They entered the house, and they were puzzled – because it was absolutely empty. He had even removed the furniture, the paintings, the statues, other things of the house ... everything was removed. The house was utterly empty.

They asked the son, "What have you done?"

He said to the father, "You just see, it is full."

He looked around. He said, "It is absolutely empty, you are befooling us."

The wise old man said, "Don't be angry with him; it is full, but it is full with something that you are not acquainted with. What he has done is that he has just purchased candles and put the candles all over the house – it is full of light."

Light is not material, it is not objective. The word 'objective' is beautiful; it means that which objects to you. You want to go through the wall. The wall will object, will prevent you; the wall is objective.

Light is immaterial.

It is a strange phenomenon on the earth. In a sense it is outside you, can be called objective, but in another sense it is not creating any objection – you can pass through it, it is immaterial.

It was thought for centuries that light had no weight; just recently they have discovered that it has weight, but it is almost negligible. When the sky is without clouds and the sun is burning hot, all the rays that fall on five square miles will have some weight that can be detected. If we could collect all those rays, they would give you a little sense of weight.

So in a way, light is part of the objective world, and in a way it is part of the non-objective world.

The old man said, "You don't understand the boy." And the boy returned most of the money. He said, "This was too much. I could have filled the house in many other dimensions also. I could have brought music into the house, which has no weight. I could have brought incense into the house – the fragrance has no weight, and it would fill the house. But I thought that would be doing too much. This is enough – and why waste your money? You take your money back; a small part of your money was enough."

Ashok, when you are in love, in a way you feel as if you are disappearing into an emptiness as far as the material world is concerned: But on the other hand, you are entering a new kind of fullness – immaterial, spiritual, not of this world.

But this is not the only world. Something transcendental, something from the beyond....

And I can see your love.

This whole month it has been growing, as if spring has come to you, new green leaves, new flowers, a new perfume, and your heart is full of new visions.

Just continue dissolving into love.

That's the meaning of disciplehood: dissolving into the love, dissolving into the presence of the master; just becoming one with his heartbeats. And songs will shower on you, and flowers of unknown, unexperienced fragrances will grow in you.

You are on the right track.

Just don't look back – and don't stop anywhere, because this is a journey that only begins but never ends.

Beloved Osho,

I wonder whether as Your disciple I can be utterly selfish, to find my way to enlightenment whatever I am doing, or do I have to fulfill a certain function for You to spread Your vision?

It has to be understood very clearly that nobody has a duty to spread my vision, my message to the people.

I hate the very word 'missionary'. These are the ugliest creatures on the earth.

I don't want to create missionaries.

You have to be utterly selfish, concentrated on only one aim: becoming enlightened.

Of course, as you become enlightened, your light will start reaching to others. My message will start vibrating through you, through your love, without any effort on your part.

It has never been said: "Be utterly selfish." All the religions of the world have been teaching, "Be altruistic," and they all have failed, because their very foundation was wrong.

You don't know what truth is, and you start spreading the message about truth. You are lying.

I have asked Christian missionaries, "What is your experience?" They don't have any experience. What they have is degrees from theological colleges. Somebody is a D. D., a doctor of divinity. Because he has written a thesis, he has become a doctor of divinity – and he knows nothing about divineness, he has never tasted anything that he can call divine. He has never had a single moment in his life when he has touched the beyond; he had no time – he was reading books and writing his doctoral thesis. He was concerned with words, not with experiences.

I lived in Jabalpur for at least twenty years, and Jabalpur has Asia's biggest Christian theological college. It prepares missionaries – that's its function.

The principal was very much interested in me. I asked him, "Be sincere: do you really feel that you have something more than the body and the mind? Have you experienced anything of the soul?"

He said, "I have read about it, and I trust that the people who have written about it are not lying."

I said, "It is possible they were also in the same position as you are, that they had read other people whom they believed could not lie – but you cannot be certain unless you experience. And what about your professors? And you are preparing three thousand missionaries per year; you are giving them degrees to go all over Asia to convert other people to Christianity. This whole game is hypocrisy. None of your teachers, none of your students has any taste of meditation; none of them has encountered God. And I think none of them is ready to be crucified like Jesus Christ."

I asked him, "Are you ready to be crucified like Jesus Christ?"

He said, "What kind of question are you asking? I have children, I have my wife, I have my old parents."

I said, "Jesus also had his old parents. And you are almost sixty; he was only thirty-three. Then why are you hanging a golden cross on a golden chain around your neck? Because as far as I understand, the neck has to be put on the cross – not that the cross is golden, hanging around your neck on a gold chain."

He said, "I was thinking that one day I would ask you to speak to my college students" – they had almost five thousand students – "but now, I have dropped that idea. You can disturb the whole thing."

And the same question, you are asking me.

I am not *converting* you.

I am trying to explain to you how to transform yourself, how to become more luminous, how to become more alert, more conscious.

And if that consciousness brings you experiences which are not available ordinarily, and those experiences have an intrinsic quality that they have to be shared, then share them. But don't try to impose any ideology on anyone.

You love me. Naturally the desire arises that others should also love me.

But the only right way is that you should come to a state that others start loving you.

I can be connected through you to others; not by your words, but by your life.

You are not to be a missionary.

You have to become a message yourself.

People should ask you, "What has happened to you? Why do we feel such a magnetic attraction towards you? Why do we feel that you are hiding some treasure from us? Why do we feel that you have moved far above our ordinary visions?"

Then share your experience; there is no need to convert anybody.

And when somebody comes on his own accord to be transformed, to learn the whole science of living in a new way, it is totally different. When you go to people to somehow convince their minds that your ideology is better than their ideology, it is possible that you may convince a few people with your ideology, but it is not conversion. They remain the same.

The Catholic, the Protestant, the Hindu, the Mohammedan, the Jew, the Communist – what is the difference in their lifestyle?

If you insult any of them, they are going to react in the same way.

I am reminded of a beautiful story.

Gautam Buddha is passing near a village which consists of high caste Brahmins only. They are very much against Gautam Buddha, they have all gathered outside the village to condemn him, to abuse him. He stands there listening to their abuse, their allegations, their lies. Even Ananda – who has been with him all these years – feels angry. Because they were born into a royal family: they were warriors; their whole training was to fight. But because Gautam Buddha is present, he controls himself; otherwise he would have killed one or two people then and there.

Gautam Buddha said to them, "You see that the sun is going to set soon, and we have to reach the other village before the sun sets. If you have not finished all that you wanted to say to me, I will make a point that when I return I set aside enough time to listen to you again. And in two days, I will be returning along the same route – so it will be very kind of you if you can wait just two days."

One man from the crowd said, "You don't seem to be disturbed at all. And we are not just saying things to you – we are abusing you, insulting you."

Gautam Buddha said, "You have come a little late. If you had come ten years before, you would not have gone back alive. I am also a warrior. There would have been bloodshed here; not a single man in this crowd would have gone back alive. But you have come a little late.

"In the village just before this village, people came with sweets and fruits. And we said, 'We eat only once a day, and we have taken our food, so it would be very kind if you would take these things back with you. We are grateful.' What do you think they did with those sweets and those fruits?"

Somebody said, "They must have distributed them amongst themselves; *they* must have eaten them."

Buddha said, "You are intelligent. Do the same: whatever you have brought, I don't accept; take it back. Because unless I accept your insult, you cannot insult me; it is a two-way affair. It is your mouth, you can say anything – but unless I accept it, you are just talking into the air. Just go home and say all these things to each other; enjoy. And I will be coming again after two days, so be ready."

They were shocked, and they could not believe – what kind of man is this?

When they moved on, Ananda said to Buddha, "This is too much. There were moments when I was going to jump and hit the man! Just because of you, I tried to control my temptation."

Buddha said – *and remember it* – he said: "What those people were saying has not hurt me. What *you* are saying hurts me. You have been with me for so many years, and yet you are not aware enough to know what to take and what not to take? Can't you discriminate?"

I want you not to become missionaries, I want you to become messages.

And that is possible only if you are utterly selfish, so that before you start helping others, you have helped yourself; before you start enlightening other people, you are enlightened yourself.

That's what I mean by being selfish.

Whatever you want to spread must be your living experience.

Beloved Osho,

These days here with You are certainly the most beautiful. Doing nothing, so much time to sit silently in the garden, in my room, and watch the trees dancing in the wind, sparkling in the sun ... so much beauty.

My mind is finally getting used to the idea of being turned off. I am so peaceful, so happy. Now, today, again going inside on this path of silence, with thoughts drifting away and emptiness surrounding me, I am aware of a tension inside me as if I am holding on to something.

My beloved master; what am I holding on to, and how do I let go?

It is not difficult to find out what you are holding on to, what your subtle tension is inside.

You are feeling peaceful, you are feeling silent, you are feeling blissful as you have never felt. Hence, side by side a fear must be lurking inside: soon you will be going from here – will this peace, this silence, this blissfulness remain a part of you? Or the moment you are away from me, will this disappear?

This fear is not only within you, it is in every disciple's mind, that when you are here it is one thing and when you go back to the marketplace, into the world, you will find it more miserable, more saddening than before because now you have something to compare it with.

Have you seen? – by the side of the road you are standing in darkness, and a car passes with its headlights on. The darkness disappears for a moment. The car is gone, but strangely enough after the car is gone the darkness is greater than it was before the car had come. You have seen the light. Now there is a comparison.

This fear is natural.

Only one thing can be done about it; and that is not to repress it but let it surface. You are repressing; that's why you are not finding what it is that is troubling you somewhere inside. Allow it to surface. Experience that fear also.

Accept the fear, and accept the challenge of the fear. Tell your mind: "It does not matter where I am. Whatever I have experienced, it is *my* experience and I can create it again."

It may have been triggered in my presence, but it is not *my* experience, it is your experience.

Let it be settled deeply in you that it is *your* experience, it has nothing to do with me. I may have been a catalytic agent, but the experience is yours.

And now, once it has happened, you can create it again anywhere in the world. Maybe in the beginning you will find it a little difficult, because you have become accustomed and associated it with my presence. But it is not dependent on my presence.

It is just as if you light a candle with another candle – but once the candle is lit, it has its own flame. Perhaps in the beginning it needed to be close enough to another flame, but once it catches the flame, it has its own, it is no longer dependent.

And when you go away, you *will* experience what I am saying – but give it a chance. Don't decide that "Now it cannot happen because the master is not here."

The master was needed to make you aware that it is something within you. Now you have seen it.

Close your eyes anywhere, and you can recreate the silence, the beauty, the bliss. You can even recreate the presence of the master – that is the most difficult part, but not impossible. It depends on how intense is your love, how deep is your trust. But no need to try it.

First try those things which you can create within yourself. And once you have created all those things then you can try the tremendously beautiful experiment of creating the presence of the master.

So don't be worried; just bring your fear to the surface: And it is not only in you, it is in everyone. It is something in the nature of things. So don't give it too much importance either; just accept it as a natural phenomenon which will disappear by your little experiments away from me.

I guarantee it will disappear, because I have guaranteed it to thousands of my *sannyasins* and it has disappeared from their lives. There is no reason why it should not disappear from your life. The principles are the same, there are no exceptions.

Beloved Osho,

I seem to be so unconscious so much of the time, so very unaware and just simply involved in life and loving living it. When You speak about the totality and intensity of the search, and how nothing else really matters, and how important it is to let nothing become a distraction, I fear I will never manage it.

In my heart I feel nothing else does matter, yet I am not living in this awareness all the time and in every situation.

Would it be good for me to try to bring this awareness to each and every moment, even if it requires intense effort? If You feel this is good for me, I will try it even though I am afraid I may lose some of the fun and spontaneity and ease of just living, and even though I don't know if I can manage it.

Maitri, the question is significant for everybody. Because I am speaking to so many people – not only those who are present here, but also to those millions who are not present here but will be hearing my words or reading my words.

It becomes a very difficult affair, because people are different in many ways. And certainly no two persons are the same.

And the danger is that you may start doing something which is not meant for you.

A simple criterion should be remembered: whatever feels good for you – blissful, peaceful, spontaneous, happening on its own accord – that is your path.

But I have to speak also to those people for whom nothing is spontaneous, for whom the most difficult thing is to relax, for whom the most impossible thing is just to sit and not to do anything. They also need every help.

To them I say, "Live with total intensity, with total effort" – because that is the easiest thing for them. And whatever is easy is close to truth.

Maitri, for you that would not be the easiest thing. You would have to make effort *against* yourself; it would not be natural, it would not be spontaneous.

You would be forcing yourself, and this will destroy the whole beauty and the peace and the silence that you are already feeling.

If you are feeling silence, peace, a beautiful energy through spontaneity, through relaxation, through let-go, then that is your way.

Everybody has to find out what is close to his heart.

I am speaking for many people of many types.

You have to find out what is right for you. If you start doing *everything* that I am saying, you will get in a mess.

You simply do that which your heart supports.

And the heart is never wrong, remember. The mind can be right, can be wrong. The heart is always right, there is no question of its being wrong.

So whenever your heart feels at ease with something, then go with it – root and all. Then don't look back and don't bother about what others are doing. Let them do *their* thing; you do *your* thing:

Because the religions of the past emphasized only one method, naturally that religion became only for one type of people. It is because of this that there are three hundred religions on the earth.

And I want only one religiousness.

All those three hundred religions have some kind of truth and some kind of validity to them. But they are specializations of a certain method, applicable to certain people – and that has made the whole world irreligious.

For example, effort is the way for Mahavira. Even to mention the word 'let-go' is to support laziness.

`Mahavira' is not his name; his name was Vardhamana. He is called Mahavira because his attitude and approach is that truth has to be conquered. It is not a love affair, it is a war. And Mahavira has won the war; that is why he is called the great warrior. 'Mahavira' means the great warrior.

Now, it creates trouble. His method is suitable only to a certain type of person – the warrior type. But because of his own teaching, his followers – who all came from the *Chhatriyas (Kshatriyas)*, the warrior race in India – had to drop their profession of being warriors, because that is violence.

Now they were in trouble – what to do? They could not be *Brahmins* because a Brahmin is only born. You cannot become a Brahmin by studying or by doing anything, there is no way. A Brahmin is only born; you cannot be converted into a Brahmin. So these people could not be Brahmins.

These people could not be *Sudras*, untouchables, because they were high caste Hindus, second only to Brahmins. They had their own pride.

The only way for them was to become businessmen. So all the Jainas in India are businessmen. They could not become cultivators, gardeners, because in cultivation or gardening you will have to cut trees and that is violence, because trees have life. So all other areas are rejected.

These business people are not trained like Mahavira. He was trained in his youth as a warrior, as a fighter, and he brought his fighting qualities to his search for truth. Now, these business people are not trained for fighting.

If somebody comes and says that truth can be purchased, they will be ready! But "truth has to be conquered"? – that just seems to be out of reach. 'Conquered' ... that is beyond their scope.

All they can do is worship Mahavira. Twenty-five centuries have passed, and Jainas have not been able to produce another man of the same caliber as Mahavira. What is the reason?

He represented one type, and he preached for one type, but it was an accident that the people who followed him were not of that type and cannot be of that type. So they have remained in a limbo, they cannot move anywhere,

Business they can do. And they have created the most beautiful temples in India, the most beautiful statues. Worship they can do. But fighting? That is simply not possible.

So a strange phenomenon ... the teacher they followed was of a different type. They were impressed by his unique quality, he was a man of steel. But his followers can simply praise him; they cannot do what their teacher has done. And this is not only with Jainas, this is the situation with every religion.

And there is no necessity that your child will be of the same type as you are. But by a certain calamity we have accepted the idea that religion comes by birth. This is simply stupid. It is as if a doctor's son becomes doctor because he is born to a doctor. He need not go to the medical college – what is the need? And if he is the son of a doctor whose wife is also a doctor, then there is no question – in his very blood and bones he is a born doctor, he needs no certificate.

It is good that we don't do this.

But in religion we *have* been doing it.

I have seen people who are born into a religion where devotion is not allowed. It is not for the devotional type, but the person *is* of the devotional type. Somebody is the type who can easily move with a negative approach, and for somebody else a negative approach is simply impossible; unless something positive is there, he cannot take a single step.

My own suggestion is that religion should not be something decided by birth; a religion should be decided by the person himself according to his feelings. Wherever he feels good, growing, wherever he feels joyous, wherever he feels a certain magnetic attraction, that is his path. It does not matter whether that is the religion he is *born into* or not; that is the religion he is *born for.*

But that is possible only if everybody is freed from religious slavery, and we allow our children to be acquainted with all kinds of religions, all kinds of methods. And if we tell them to feel, to move with different kinds of people: "Go to different temples, go to different schools, go to different masters, and feel your way." And wherever he feels that this is his nourishment, then the parents have to bless him to go on that way.

It does not matter if you feel nourished in the company of a Mohammedan Sufi, it does not matter if you feel nourished in the company of a Buddhist monk; the whole question should be decided by your own heart.

And the heart never leads you wrong. If you allow it, it will give you clear-cut indications that you are on the right path. Peace, silence, bliss, benediction – all will be coming more and more, and the scope will become wider and wider.

Beloved Osho,

Who is the blessed one?

The one who is asleep in you is the blessed one, but unfortunately he is sleeping and snoring.

He has to be awakened, and the moment your sleeping consciousness becomes wakeful you start feeling blissfulness.

The highest peak of your bliss makes you feel to go beyond humanity. That is the moment of being the blessed one; you have become part of the universal blissfulness.

But people are so asleep.

I have suffered so much from people's sleep.

Because I used to travel continually in India; mostly I was in an air-conditioned coupe, but sometimes there was another person in the coupe also. And sometimes a coupe was not available so there were four persons.

Once it happened, I was coming from Calcutta in a four-person room. And I have seen many snoring people, but I will not forget those three fellows.

They had a certain harmony: one would snore and the other two would remain silent, and then as he would stop, the second would snore louder than the first and the other two would remain silent. And as the second would stop, the third would snore loudest of all, and the other two would remain silent.

And the circle went on.

I heard this for one hour and then I said, "This is impossible. I don't want to interfere in anybody's life, but these three people are interfering in my life."

So as the third stopped, I snored so loudly that all three became awake.

And they saw me snoring with open eyes, so they could not believe ... they could not believe it. They looked at each other like, "What kind of man is this? His eyes are open."

And I was not blinking my eyes.

All three got up from their seats and came close to me.

I said, "Listen, if you want to sleep, stop this harmony that is going on. Otherwise, I will not allow *any* of you to sleep."

One of them said, "But you are awake and you are snoring?"

I said, "What else to do? – because I cannot sleep, so the question of sleeping and *then* snoring does not arise. You don't allow me to sleep! First let me sleep. Then perhaps I may fall into the harmony, something may happen; but first let me sleep. And how are you managing?"

They said, "We three are brothers."

I said, "You are great brothers."

They said, "What to do? – it is such a difficult matter, even in our family. Our wives don't sleep in our rooms; we three brothers have to sleep in one room. So, slowly, slowly, a certain harmony has arisen."

I said, "That's perfectly good; but in just one night it will be very difficult for me to get into the harmony. Something has to be done."

So we had to come to a conclusion that those three fellows would play cards while I slept for a few hours, and then they would have their harmony and I would sit and listen.

But listening to them was also beautiful, because ... how were they managing any sleep?

Everybody is carrying the blessed one, but it needs to be awakened.

The blessed one is not a certain talent.

It is not like being a musician: a few people are musicians but *everybody* cannot be; a few people are painters but everybody cannot be; a few people are poets, dancers, actors, writers – these are talents.

The blessed one is not a question of talent.

It is your very nature. It is your self-nature, it is your intrinsic quality.

It is up to you how long you want to be miserable and asleep – you are free.

The moment you decide that enough is enough, you will have the same experiences as any Gautam Buddha or Ramakrishna or Raman Maharshi – these are not talented people. Kabir or Raidas or Farid – these are not talented people, they are just ordinary human beings.

But as far as their blissfulness is concerned, they have reached to the same peak as Gautam Buddha.

It is your birthright.

•••

3

MASTER AND DISCIPLE: A MYSTERY BEYOND EXPLAINING

Beloved Osho,

*Every time when people ask me, "What is Bhagwan in your life?" –
I answer that You are my master. But the people don't understand, even
if I try to explain. What is the reason for it? Why can't I explain it
with success?*

L ife is beautiful because there is so much which cannot be explained.

It would have been a disaster if life consisted only of things which can be explained.

Just think for a moment: if everything could be explained, then there would be no mystery, then there would be no poetry, then there would be no secret. Then everything would be utterly flat and boring.

Life is not a boredom because there are dimensions in it that you can go on exploring, yet you can never come to explanations. You can experience much, yet even that which you have experienced cannot be translated into words.

You fall in love. Since the very first man, millions of people must have fallen in love; yet love is still a mystery, you cannot reduce it to knowledge.

The moment you try to reduce it to knowledge, it slips out of your hands. And it is good that it is so miraculous that generation after generation, millions of people go through the experience; they know what it is, yet they cannot say what it is.

All that can be experienced is not necessarily explainable, and all that can be explained is not necessarily experienceable.

Mathematics can be explained easily, but there is no corresponding experience. Science can be explained easily, but even the greatest scientist is not transformed by his knowledge. But an anonymous poet not only gives birth to poetry, he also goes through a deep revolution, a rebirth. His poetry is not just a composition of words; it is the juice of his very life.

The greatest poets have not been able to explain their own poetry.

Once Coleridge was asked by a professor of literature.... The professor was teaching at the university and he came across a point in one of Coleridge's poems where he was doubtful about the meaning. He was a sincere man. He told the students, "You will have to wait at least one day. Coleridge lives in my neighborhood; I can ask him exactly what he means."

The professor went to Coleridge that evening. Coleridge said, "You have come a little late."

He said, "What do you mean a little late? You are still alive."

Coleridge said, "It is not a question of my being alive or not. When I wrote these lines, two persons knew the meaning; now only one knows."

Naturally, the professor inferred that that one person could not be anyone else but Coleridge.

He said, "So I have not come too late. Tell me what the meaning is."

Coleridge said, "You have not yet got the point. When I wrote these lines, two persons knew the meaning – Coleridge and God. Now only God knows!

"I myself have been wondering. Many times I have read it and wondered – what is the meaning? It is groovy! – but very slippery. You feel that you are just about to catch it and it is gone just like a breeze. I am sorry. I have certainly written these lines, and I know there *is* some meaning, and I *feel* it, but you will have to forgive me. I cannot even explain it to myself, how can I explain it to you?"

It is not only so about poetry: Anything significant in life.

Picasso used to get very angry whenever anybody would ask the meaning of his paintings. And he was not an angry man. He was a very beautiful, loving person. But the moment you ask the meaning of his painting, you have touched him from the wrong side.

He would immediately get very angry. He would say, "This is strange. Nobody asks a roseflower what its meaning is. Nobody asks the stars what their meaning is. Nobody asks a bird on the wing what its meaning is. Nobody asks a sunrise or a sunset what its meaning is. People simply enjoy the beauty; nobody bothers about the meaning. Why are people after me? I am a poor painter. All that I can say is that it is beautiful. But that is not its meaning, it is its impact on a sensitive being."

Meaning is rational. And the experience of mystery is supra-rational.

Your question is significant, and it must be the question of many other disciples.

People ask you what the relationship is between you and me.

Just to say that I am your master neither satisfies them nor satisfies you.

How can it satisfy them when it does not satisfy even you? – because it is not just a relationship like somebody is your father and somebody is your mother and somebody is your brother. Once you have said that somebody is your father, everything is explained. Nobody bothers you anymore, that "What do you mean by father?" and....

The relationship with the master is not of the same category as all other relationships. It is intrinsically different.

It is love, but not only love.

It is love with a center of trust.

Love alone is unexplainable, and now it has joined hands with an even greater mystery. Trust is absolutely something of another world.

In this world, there is distrust in everybody. Even in people who love each other, there is no trust. There are friends who can, if there is need, die for each other – but there is no trust.

In the Middle Ages it used to happen....

A very strange and ugly thing was in existence in Europe. Whenever a warrior would go to war, he would put a lock on his wife so that she could not make love to anybody, and take the key with him. A strange device it was ... those locks are still exhibited in the museums of Europe.

You cannot even trust your wife! And if you cannot trust your wife, do you think a master key cannot be found? The goldsmiths who made the locks also made extra keys!

One prince was going to war. His only fear was about his beautiful wife. He was afraid that if the key were lost in the war then for the rest of his life he wouldn't be able to make love to his own wife. So he thought it would be better to give the key to one of his best friends.

They were so close that they would have died for each other, so there was no question of distrust.

He gave his friend the key and told him, "When I come back I will take it back. So keep it safe."

He had gone not more than a half mile out of the town on his horse when he heard a fast horse approaching him from behind. He looked back, and his friend was coming, shouting, "Wait!"

He said, "What has happened?" Just five minutes ago he had left him perfectly healthy, and there had been no problem.

The friend said, "You gave me the wrong key!"

In this world, there is no trust at all.

When love is joined with trust, it becomes even more difficult to explain it. It becomes more mysterious.

And thirdly, as love and trust grow to their optimum, something comes which can only be called 'surrender'. It is not a good word, but there is no other word as a substitute.

Surrender makes the whole thing absolutely not of this world. You cannot give any reason, you cannot give any explanation. The only way is: whoever asks, tell him that it is something like a thirsty man finding water in the desert. His every fiber is just thirst, and the water quenches all thirst. A great peace descends.

The master is not a person.

The master is only a presence.

If you are thirsty enough for the unknown, you can drink out of this presence and be quenched.

Anybody who asks you the question, tell him, "Come with me. There are a few things which cannot be explained, but I can take you to the place where perhaps you may also experience them. Your question itself shows that there is some interest in you – perhaps a deep, hidden desire.

"Who knows? – it may become aflame in the presence of the master. Who knows? surrounded by disciples and their love and their trust and their surrender, and the presence of the master, something may transpire in you. One thing is certain: if something transpires in you, you will become dumb the way I am dumb."

Accept your dumbness, but create a quest in the person who is asking only for a verbal answer. Use that situation. A verbal answer is of no use. You just say, "I have experienced something, which is untranslatable into any language, but I can take you to the river. You yourself can drink. Your experience will be the only explanation."

And I repeat again: Life is beautiful because there are so many unexplainable dimensions to it. That is its richness. If everything is explained, all juice will be lost; you will be fed up, bored to death with a life which is explained.

What transpires between a master and a disciple is one of the peaks of unexplainable experiences. Don't destroy it with any explanation.

It is a crime to destroy the unexplainable by bringing it to the level of explanations, because you have killed. It is almost like a bird on the wing in the sky ... it is so beautiful in its freedom; the whole sky belongs to him, all the stars belong to him ... no limits, no barriers.

You can catch hold of the bird; you can make a beautiful golden cage and you can put the bird in the cage. But remember, it is not the same bird that was flying in freedom in the sky under the stars. Factually it is the same bird, but spiritually no – because where is the freedom and where are the stars? Where is the sky? Your golden cage cannot replace what you have taken away from the bird. It has lost its soul.

The same happens when you try to explain something which is unexplainable. You bring it into the cage of language, of words – beautiful words, but the soul has disappeared.

Don't do it. I know it feels a little awkward when somebody asks and you cannot answer – you feel embarrassed.

It is better to feel embarrassed. But don't commit a crime against the mysteries of life.

Tell the person, "1 am feeling embarrassed because I cannot say it.

Not that I don't want to say it – I would have loved to say it to you but I cannot, because saying it means killing it.

"I can take you to the window from where you can see the open sky, I can take you to the man. Perhaps your heart will start dancing in the same way my heart dances within me. And in deep silence, you will understand what it means to me. But only when it starts to mean something to you."

People will be asking you many questions. Use their questions to invite them towards the same light, towards the same bliss, towards the same truth.

Don't answer – because you cannot answer, and whatever you say will fall flat.

Resist the temptation of being knowledgeable. Accept your inarticulateness. But invite the person.

Perhaps out of ten, one may turn up. And one never knows – by coming here, he may turn on!

Beloved Osho,

I am old, and had been a Buddhist for over thirty years before I came to Poona. But still I feel as if I am at the beginning, confused with lots of doubts.

On the other hand, something inside me knows about Your silence, and that something is not irritated at all. It is like a robe of trust. But I am not able to believe. Could You please say something about the difference between trust and belief.

Trust and belief have a very similar appearance, but they are diametrically opposite realities.

Belief is a false coin. It pretends to be real; it tries to play the role of trust. Millions of people are caught in the net of belief, because it is cheap.

Trust is costly, very costly.

Trust is costly because it is risky, it is dangerous. It means you are opening yourself, becoming vulnerable to somebody who can do you harm. You are dropping all your defense measures. You will be defenseless — you can be exploited, cheated, destroyed.

Everybody has a defense system around himself, just to protect himself from others.

Life is competitive. Everybody is running after the same goals, and you cannot remain loving, compassionate, kind, in a competitive world or you are going to be a failure.

In this competitive world, the people who succeed are the people who are ready to sacrifice anybody, to destroy anybody. They go on climbing on people as if people were stepping stones. They care about only one thing, and that is success. Naturally, everybody has to be ready not to be trampled, killed.

Trust means going against the current of the competitive world. In the competitive world, trust is simply impossible.

Machiavelli wrote one of the most significant treatises on diplomacy, *The Prince*. Strangely enough, his great great granddaughter is a *sannyasin* – Machiavelli would have never dreamed that his blood would one day trust somebody.

Machiavelli has written in *The Prince* – it is a small treatise for every politician, maxims to be followed if you want to succeed – "Don't trust anybody, but let everybody believe that you trust them. Don't say anything to a friend that you would not say to an enemy – because no one knows, the friend may turn into your enemy tomorrow. Don't say anything against your enemy that you would not say against your friend– because in this competitive world, the person who is an enemy may become a friend, the person who is a friend may become an enemy.

"Basically, keep yourself completely closed and secretive. If you say something, say it in such a way that it can be interpreted either way, for or against. Don't say anything which has only a single meaning, because every day you will have to face a new reality and you will have to change your meaning."

Machiavelli is the real leader of the world – not Jesus Christ or Gautam Buddha. It is a strange world. Here, the *real* leaders are not worshipped, but they are followed. Here, the *unreal* leaders are worshipped ... but not followed.

When love and trust meet, their ultimate byproduct is – surrender. You relax into the master, into his being, without holding anything.

It is certainly only for those who are ready to take a risk.

But belief is very cheap. Everybody is a believer – somebody is a Hindu, somebody is a Mohammedan, somebody is a Christian. Belief comes in all sizes, all shapes, all colors – you can choose. And you don't have to pay anything for it. Generally you get it with your mother's milk, free of charge.

Secondly, belief is always in an idea, and trust is always in a presence.

That is a very delicate difference.

Belief is theoretical.

Trust is existential.

You can change your belief without any trouble; it is just like changing your clothes. From a Hindu, you can become a Christian;

from a Christian, you can become a Mohammedan; from a Mohammedan, you can become a Communist. There is no problem, because belief is only of the mind. If anything is more convincing, more logical, you can change it. It has no roots in your heart.

Belief is like plastic flowers, which look like flowers from far away. They don't have any roots, they don't need any care – no manure, no chemicals, no watering, no gardening, nothing is needed. And they are permanent people, they can remain with you your whole life long – because they were never born, so they will never die. They are manufactured. Unless you destroy them, they will remain.

Trust is a real rose. It has roots, and roots go deep into your heart and into your being. Belief is just in the head.

Trust is in the heart, in your deeper world of being. To change trust is almost impossible – it has never happened, it is not known to have happened in the whole of history. If you trust, you trust; there is no possibility of its changing. And it goes on growing because it has roots. It never remains static; it is dynamic, it is a living force, it goes on growing new foliage, new flowers, new branches.

Belief is a dead thing, a plastic flower – it never grows. Hindus may have believed in a certain thing for ten thousand years – it is still there, the same; it never grows.

"The cow is the mother." Hindus have believed it for ten thousand years. The belief has not grown even to include the fact that the bull is your father. It is static. And if you mention to any Hindu that the bull is his father then he will *become* a bull, and prove that certainly the bull *is* his father! – but he will not believe it. He will behave exactly like a bull, but he will not accept the fact.

All beliefs are old, all beliefs are dead. No belief grows even a single leaf.

Belief is ideological, philosophical, but it is not a force that transforms your being. It can make you a great scholar, it can make you a great philosopher, theologian – but it can never make you a new man, young and fresh; it cannot give you any experience. It can bring you degrees from the universities and awards and Nobel prizes; it can do everything.

But it will not change anything in your interior; it will remain empty.

The question is even more important because it is coming from a person who has been a Buddhist for thirty years.

After being a Buddhist for thirty years, the person comes to me, feels a certain trust in me, falls in love. Naturally, there is a conflict which is bound to happen. His mind is full of thirty years of Buddhist ideology – that is the belief system – and the heart is growing fresh sprouts of trust. The person is bound to be in a great difficulty: The beliefs are pulling in one direction and the trust is moving in another direction.

The beliefs have a certain weight because they are thirty years old, but the trust – although it is new – has a force of its own because it is alive. The beliefs are thirty-year-old corpses. They have weight, but they don't have any force. The person is bound to be split.

Things can be solved very easily.

The first thing to remember is: if Buddhism was enough, there would have been no need to come to me. Being a Buddhist for thirty years has not done anything to you. You can be a Buddhist for thirty lives, but a belief never changes your reality. The length of time makes no difference.

So the first question you have to ask yourself is why, after thirty years, you had to seek and search for some new source, for some new light, for some new indication.

If you are courageous, you need not get into a conflict; you can simply see that those thirty years have gone to waste. But what is gone is gone; now don't waste any more time on it.

And remember: I am not saying that Buddha is wrong.

I am simply saying that Buddha was right only to those people who could drink out of his presence, for whom he was a master.

But for you, he is only a belief.

It is better to get rid of those thirty years and whatever information you have collected in you, because that is a burden and a hindrance in your spiritual growth.

If you can dare not to be a Buddhist, I promise you that there is a possibility of your being a *buddha*. Why be a Buddhist when there is a possibility of being a *buddha*? Why settle for such dead theories when living waters are available?

'To be a *buddha* is a beauty.

To be a Buddhist is stupidity.

Buddha was not a Buddhist, remember; he never heard the word. Nobody called him a Buddhist.

Jesus was never a Christian. So one thing is certain, that no Christian remaining a Christian can find the experience that Jesus found. If any Christian wants to experience what Jesus experienced, the first thing to do is to get rid of Christianity because Jesus was not a Christian.

Your belief system has to be completely thrown out, so that your juices are not divided and your whole energy moves into your trust.

Your trust is growing, but under a heavy burden, under a tension. It can grow in a relaxed way, under open sky. Just say goodbye to those beliefs that you have been carrying, and let your trust grow.

What Buddha has been to his disciples, his theories cannot be.

Theories are mere words. They don't have the charm and the grace and the charisma; they don't have that magnetism.

And when you are here and the possibility is available for you to become awakened, to become a *buddha*, I don't think that it is a bad bargain ... dropping Buddhist theories in favor of becoming Gautam Buddha himself.

In twenty-five centuries, how many *buddhas* have been produced by the Buddhists?

One English Buddhist – Bhikku Dharm Rakshita, a very devoted man – dropped Christianity, was converted to Buddhism and became one of the topmost scholars of Buddhist literature. He had an *ashram* in Kalimpong. He used to go once in a while to attend Buddhist conferences, and he made it a point that whenever he came down from the Himalayas he would find me and come to be with me for a day or two.

He was an internationally known Buddhist scholar. His books are rare as far as the accuracy of his translations is concerned.

I used to ask him, "Dharm Rakshita, you have devoted almost fifty years to learning Buddhist theology, translating Buddhist literature – but have you got any taste of *buddhahood*?"

And tears would come to his eyes. He would say, "Please, don't ask that question. You are the only person who asks that. Nobody else seems to be interested. They ask about literature, they ask about principles, philosophies and everything, but nobody asks, 'Has fifty years' concentrated effort brought anything to your being? – or has it brought only a dozen books and world fame? Are you satisfied?' "

One night he said to me, "You met me too late. I am old, I have wasted my whole life. And now it is very difficult for me to drop all that garbage that I learned with great effort, and to begin from ABC, from the very scratch. But whenever I can manage it, I just come to be near you. And whenever I am near you.... I don't know how it would have been to be with Gautam Buddha, but I feel it must have been something like this – the same taste.

"Now it is too late for me to change, but at least at the very end of my life I will not be dying just a scholar, I will be dying as a seeker. I could not do that in this life, but you have created a thirst. Perhaps in my next life I may not get lost in the jungle of theories, and I may try to enter into myself."

You have a rare opportunity here.

Nothing like this has ever existed in the world before. Because I don't have any prejudice – you can become a Christ here, you can become a Buddha here, you can become a Mahavira, you can become a Lao Tzu. I don't have any prejudice because I know these are only different names. Behind them is the same universal consciousness.

So don't be bothered about your beliefs; just drop them.

Trust is enough, more than enough. For your pilgrimage, it is enough nourishment.

Beloved Osho,

Inside of me there seem to be so many questions, but when I try to ask You one of them, they all seem to be gone, and I don't know even if I really wanted to ask You something. But still the feeling of question remains.

Please, can You explain where this feeling comes from?

It is very simple.
You don't have a question; you have a quest. And you are not aware of the distinction.

Your quest is not clear to you, it is clouded. You think perhaps there is some question – so you make many questions and they disappear but you are left with a vague feeling that something similar to a question is still there. What is it?

All questions are like leaves.

The quest is like the roots.

You are fortunate, because at first people have to ask thousands of questions; then, by and by, one by one, the leaves disappear. Then branches come, then the trunk, and then finally they realize that the real thing is the quest.

You are fortunate that you have only roots. But with roots the difficulty is that they are always underground, so you don't see where they are. You try somehow to make questions, but they disappear because they are not connected with your roots.

A quest is the most significant thing for a seeker.

A quest means you want to know, you want to experience, you want to be the truth itself.

A question wants to be answered.

A quest wants to become the answer itself.

Questions are many; the answer is one.

And you are in a position ... if you simply meditate, you will not come across a question, you will come across the answer. And the answer is not something separate from you. You are the answer.

Just go to your very center. It is there for you, waiting for thousands of lives. Don't let it wait anymore. Sometimes it also gets impatient. Because of that impatience, it starts creating questions.

Questions only show impatience.

But your position is very clear: you don't need to ask anything; you simply have to go deeper and deeper into silence, and you will find it.

Beloved Osho,

Before coming into contact with You, Professor Joshi of Kathmandu was spiritually guided by a Buddhist lama.

This lama left his family and village when he was young and traveled for forty years in Tibet, Burma and Thailand, meditating and seeking truth. At the age of sixty, one evening the lama quietly returned to his village and joined the family and his old life. But his grace and silence attracted many seekers, and now he is famous as an "avatari lama."

The professor was highly impressed by the lama, and out of love presented him with Your book, Antar Yantra.

The lama could not read Hindi or English, so he requested Mr Joshi to read some passages to him and to show him your picture. When he saw your picture, the lama said: "Osho comes from the land where I go every day in my meditation. This time He has come with full glory, (sixteen kalas) – which happens only in the incarnation of Krishna or Buddha. Now there is no need to come to me for guidance; follow Osho, He is the right master."

Osho, how can people see so much just in Your picture, which we disciples cannot realize even after such a long association?

Arun, it is not a question of long association:
It is a question of deep insight.

You don't have that meditative perspective. You can see only what the ordinary eyes can see.

But as a person becomes more meditative, he starts growing his sensitivities to such depth and such height that he is able to see things which are invisible to us.

Life is not only what is available to our five senses.

Just think.... For example, if you were all blind, you would never come to know that there is something like light – although the light will be all around you. But just the existence of light is not enough; you need something to perceive it.

One fact scientists have been concerned about is that on at least fifty thousand planets there is a possibility of life. One thing is certain: that on these different planets, life must have grown in different ways – because the climate would be different, the whole situation would be different. It is possible that on some planet there may be animals who have more than five senses. Right now it is only a hypothetical question, but it is significant; the possibility is there.

If there are animals on some planets who have seven senses or eight senses, then they must be able to perceive two or three things more than we can perceive. And we cannot even imagine what those things might be – because even in imagination, we can only imagine that which we have seen. We cannot even dream about it, because our dreams are only reflections. You cannot be so creative in your dreams to create something new: all that will be reflected are those five senses. Before x-rays were developed, we had no idea that there are rays which can enter into your body and photograph your insides.

The people who have been working on meditation for centuries have come to know many things, but because they are not scientists they have never tried to prove them objectively.

For example, in the East it has been known for centuries that a man of meditation can see if somebody is going to die within six months or not. And the thing is so simple that it need not be even a question of meditation; you yourself can know whether you are going to die within six months or not. The day you stop seeing the tip of your nose, that means only six months are left – because at the time a person dies, his eyes turn up, and they start turning up six months before that, very slowly, very slowly. From six months beforehand till his death, he cannot see the tip of his nose: Now, that is known to villagers who have no meditation or meditative understanding.

The lama has been meditating for forty years. He can see in my picture things which you cannot see.

I am reminded of Ramakrishna. A painter made his portrait, and he brought the painting to show Ramakrishna – to see whether he liked it or not. The disciples were also gathered there.

Ramakrishna looked at the painting and touched the feet of the painting. His disciples – Vivekananda and others – felt embarrassed: "What to do with our master? – because he does such things that even we look like fools. Now it is his own picture, and he is touching its feet. We had no idea that he would do this; otherwise, we would have prevented him. And now he has done it, and people are laughing and smiling and looking at each other."

There were many observers there who were not disciples. They said, "They think this man is a realized soul? He seems to be insane! Even an insane person will not touch his own feet; at least he will recognize that 'This is my own portrait; I cannot touch its feet.'"

The painter was also shocked, but he was not a disciple. So he gathered courage and asked Ramakrishna, "I cannot believe my eyes. This is your own portrait and you are touching your own feet! It looks a little awkward."

And Ramakrishna's eyes were full of tears of joy. He said, "*it* is my picture, I know, but I am not touching the feet because it is my picture. I am touching the feet because you have caught my state of *samadhi* in the picture. And when I see a picture of someone in *samadhi* ... it does not matter whether that picture is of me or somebody else — that is irrelevant. What matters is that the picture is of a self-realized consciousness, then I have to touch its feet. And I cannot see why you are all looking so embarrassed."

Now they all felt *more* embarrassed: "We are such idiots. We don't understand; we should at least keep quiet. If we don't understand, then it is better not to show any emotion. He has done something which nobody has done before, but his reason is so valid."

Arun, the lama must be going well in his meditations.

If he can see what he has seen in my picture, that validates that he is on the right path, that his meditation is bringing flowers, that he is very close to the home.

Beloved Osho,

I have heard You saying, "I love." I have heard You saying "I hate." What do You mean?

Osho, tell me the truth, for my feeling is that there is nothing up there — not even love, not even compassion.

D o I have to tell you the truth?

It is a little bit difficult for me because it is not my habit ... but the truth is there is no love, no hate.

Up there is absolute silence.

•••

4

RISING IN LOVE...
A PARTNERSHIP IN
MEDITATION

Beloved Osho,

I'm experiencing more and more a harmony, a quietness, an ease, an abundance in myself, moments in which I feel so vast and rich, like the universe, and so close to You. I dive into it and disappear, and see that this again was just an opening, a door to another dimension on this ongoing, never-ending journey You are taking me, my beloved master. And I can find no words to express how much I feel, that I can be with You.

Being together with a man I find these most beautiful and precious moments so rarely; it seems most of the time is wasted in loving and finding ourselves and each other. Why is it so difficult for me to be in this harmony together with a man, and even take him with me into this unknown? Or is it something which can happen just between You and me?

There are a few very fundamental things to be understood.
First, a man and a woman are on the one hand halves of the other and, on the other hand, opposite polarities.

Their being opposites attracts them to each other. The farther away they are, the deeper will be the attraction; the more different from each other they are, the more will be the charm and beauty and attraction. But there lies the whole problem.

When they come close, they want to come closer, they want to merge into each other, they want to become one, a harmonious whole – but their whole attraction depends on opposition, and the harmony will depend on dissolving the opposition.

Unless a love affair is very conscious, it is going to create great anguish, great trouble.

All lovers are in trouble.

The trouble is not personal; it is in the very nature of things. They would not have been attracted to each other ... they call it falling in love. They cannot give any reason why they have such a tremendous pull towards each other. They are not even conscious of the underlying causes; hence a strange thing happens: the happiest lovers are those who never meet.

Once they meet, the same opposition that created the attraction becomes a conflict. On each small point, their attitudes are different, their approaches are different. Although they speak the same language, they cannot understand each other.

One of my friends was talking to me about his wife and their continuous conflict. I said, "It seems you cannot understand each other."

He said, "What to say about *under*standing her, I cannot even *stand* her!" And it was a love marriage. The parents of both were opposed to it; they belonged to two different religions, their societies were opposed. But they fought against everybody and got married – just to find that they had entered into a constant struggle.

The way a man looks at the world is different from a woman.

For example, a man is interested in faraway things – in the future of humanity, in the faraway stars, whether there are living beings on other planets or not.

A woman simply giggles at the whole nonsense. She is only interested in a very small, closed circle – in the neighbors, in the family, in who is cheating his wife, whose wife has fallen in love with the chauffeur. Her interest is very local and very human. She is not worried about reincarnation; neither is she concerned about life after death. Her concern is more pragmatic. She is concerned with the present, here and now.

Man is never here and now. He is always somewhere else. He has strange preoccupations – reincarnation, life after death.

If both partners are conscious of the fact that it is a meeting of opposites, that there is no need to make it a conflict, then it is a great opportunity to understand the totally opposite point of view and absorb it. Then the life of a man and woman together can become a beautiful harmony. Otherwise, it is continuous fight.

There are holidays. One cannot continue to fight twenty-four hours a day; one needs a little rest too – a rest to get ready for a new fight.

But it is one of the strangest phenomena that for thousands of years men and women have been living together, yet they are strangers: They go on giving birth to children, but still they remain strangers. The feminine approach and the masculine approach are so opposed to each other that unless a conscious effort is made, unless it becomes your meditation, there is no hope of having a peaceful life.

It is one of my deep concerns: how to make love and meditation so involved in each other that each love affair automatically becomes a partnership in meditation – and each meditation makes you so conscious that you need not fall in love, you can rise in love. You can find a friend consciously, deliberately.

You feel a deep harmony with me, moments of peace, love and silence, and naturally the question has arisen in you that if this is possible with me, why is it not possible with the man you love?

The difference has to be understood.

You love me, but you don't love me in the same way you love your husband, your wife. Your love towards me is not biological; with me your love is a totally different phenomenon – it is of the spirit, not of the body.

And secondly, you are connected with me because of your search for truth. My relationship with you is that of meditation.

Meditation is the only bridge between me and you.

Your love will deepen as your meditation deepens, and vice-versa: as your meditation blossoms, your love will also blossom.

But it is on a totally different level.

With your husband, you are not connected in meditation. You never sit silently for one hour together just to feel each other's consciousness.

Either you are fighting or you are making love, but in both cases, you are related with the body, the physical part, the biology, the hormones.

You are not related with the innermost core of the other. Your souls remain separate.

In the temples and in the churches and in the courts, only your bodies are married. Your souls are miles apart.

While you are making love to your man – even in those moments – neither are you there, nor is your man there. Perhaps he is thinking of Cleopatra, Noorjahan, Mumtaj Mahal. You are also thinking....

And perhaps that's why every woman keeps her eyes closed – not to see her husband's face, not to get disturbed. She is thinking of Alexander the Great, Ivan the Terrible. And looking at her husband, everything falls apart. He looks just like a mouse.

Mulla Nasruddin and his wife were quarreling one morning. She said, "Outside the house you walk as if you are a lion, and inside the house you look just like a mouse."

Mulla Nasruddin said, "That is absolutely wrong. Put yourself right: I am not a mouse, I am a mousetrap. *You* are a mouse. Mousetraps don't run after mice to catch hold of them. The mice themselves come and get caught, and that's how it happened with us."

Mulla Nasruddin was not courageous enough to approach this woman. He was afraid from the very beginning.

Every man is afraid because he has seen what has happened to his father, what has happened to his grandfather. He has seen what is happening to every neighbor. Every man is afraid.

Mulla was very much afraid; he never approached any woman. It was this woman who caught him. So he said, "Remember' – I am a mousetrap, that is true, but I was just sitting in my place. *You* got into *me*, it is your responsibility."

But it does not matter who catches who, who takes the initiative.

Even in those beautiful moments which should be sacred, meditative, of deep silence ... even then you are not alone with your beloved. There is a crowd. Your mind is thinking of somebody else, your wife's mind is thinking of somebody else. Then what you are doing is just robot-like, mechanical. Some biological force is enslaving you, and you call it love.

I have heard that early in the morning, a drunkard on the beach saw a man doing pushups. The drunkard walked around him, looked very closely from here and from there, and finally said, "I should not interfere in such an intimate affair, but I have to tell you that your girlfriend has gone. Now don't exercise unnecessarily – first get up and find where she is!"

That seems to be the situation. When you are making love, is your woman really there? Is your man really there? Or are you just doing a ritual – something which has to be done, a duty to be fulfilled?

If you want a harmonious relationship with your man, you will have to learn to be more meditative.

Love alone is not enough.

Love alone is blind; meditation gives it eyes. Meditation gives it understanding. And once your love is both love and meditation, you become fellow travelers. Then it is no longer an ordinary relationship between husband and wife. Then it becomes a friendliness on the path towards discovering the mysteries of life.

Man alone, woman alone, will find the journey very tedious and very long ... as they have found it in the past. Because seeing this continuous conflict, all the religions decided that those who wanted to seek should renounce the other – the monks should be celibate, the nuns should be celibate. But in five thousand years of history, how many monks and how many nuns have become realized souls? You cannot even give me names enough to count on ten fingers. And millions of monks and nuns of all religions – Buddhist, Hindu, Christian, Mohammedan.... What has happened?

The path is not so long. The goal is not that far away. But even if you want to go to your neighbor's house, you will need both your legs. Just jumping on one leg, how far can you go?

I am introducing a totally new vision, that men and women together in deep friendship, in a loving, meditative relationship, as organic wholes, can reach the goal any moment they want. Because the goal is not outside you; it is the center of the cyclone, it is the innermost part of your being. But you can find it only when you are whole, and you cannot be whole without the other.

Man and woman are two parts of one whole.

So rather than wasting time in fighting, try to understand each other. Try to put yourself in the place of the other; try to see as a man sees, try to see as a woman sees. And four eyes are always better than two eyes – you have a full view; all four directions are available to you.

But one thing has to be remembered: that without meditation, love is destined to fail; there is no possibility of its being a success. You can pretend and you can deceive others, but you cannot deceive yourself. You know deep down that all the promises love had given to you have remained unfulfilled.

Only with meditation does love start taking on new colors, new music, new songs, new dances – because meditation gives you the insight to understand the polar opposite, and in that very understanding the conflict disappears.

All the conflict in the world is because of misunderstanding. You say something, your wife understands something else. Your wife says something, you understand something else.

I have seen couples who have lived together for thirty or forty years; still, they seem to be as immature as they were on their first day together. Still the same complaint: "She doesn't understand what I am saying." Forty years being together and you have not been able to figure out some way that your wife can understand exactly what you are saying, and you can understand exactly what she is saying.

But I think there is no possibility for it to happen except through meditation, because meditation gives you the qualities of silence, awareness, a patient listening, a capacity to put yourself in the other's position.

It is possible with me: I am not concerned with the trivia of your life. You are here basically to listen and understand. You are here to grow spiritually. Naturally there is no question of conflict, and the harmony arises without any effort.

You can love me with totality, because with me your relationship is of meditation. With any other man or with any other woman, if you want to live in harmony you will have to bring the same atmosphere and the same climate that you have brought here.

Things are not impossible, but we have not tried the right medicine.

I would like you to be reminded that the word 'medicine' comes from the same root as 'meditation'. Medicine cures your body; meditation cures your soul. Medicine heals the material part of you; meditation heals the spiritual part of you.

People are living together and their spirits are full of wounds; hence, small things hurt them so much.

Mulla Nasruddin was asking me, "What to do? – whatever I say I am misunderstood, and immediately there is trouble."

I said, "Try one thing: just sit silently, don't say anything."

The next day, I saw him in more despair than ever. I said, "What happened?"

He said, "I should not ask you for advice. Every day we used to fight and quarrel, but it was just verbal. Yesterday, because of your advice, I got beaten!"

I said, "What happened?"

He said, "I just sat there silent. She asked many questions, but I was determined to remain silent. She said, 'So you are not going to speak?' I remained silent. So she started hitting me with things! And she was very angry. She said, 'Things have gone from bad to worse. At least we used to talk to each other; now even we are not on speaking terms!'"

I said, "This is really bad."

He said, "You are saying *bad*? The whole neighborhood gathered, and they all started asking, 'What happened? Why aren't you speaking?' And somebody suggested: 'It seems he is possessed by some evil spirit.'

"I thought, my God, now they are going to take me to some idiot who will beat me and try to drive the evil spirit out. I said, 'Wait! I'm not possessed by any evil spirit, I'm simply not speaking because to say anything triggers a fight: I say something, then she has to say something, and then I have to say something, and nobody knows where it is going to end.'

"I was simply meditating silently, doing no harm to anybody – and suddenly the whole neighborhood was against me!"

People are living without any understanding. Hence, whatsoever they do is going to end in disaster.

If you love a man, meditation will be the best present that you can give to him.

If you love a woman, then the Kohinoor is nothing; meditation will be a far more precious gift – and it will make your life sheer joy.

We are potentially capable of sheer joy, but we don't know how to manage it.

Alone, we are at the most sad.

Together, it becomes really hell.

Even a man like Jean-Paul Sartre, a man of great intelligence, has to say that the other is hell, that to be alone is better, you cannot make it with the other. He became so pessimistic that he said it is impossible to make it with the other, the other is hell. Ordinarily, he is right.

With meditation the other becomes your heaven.

But Jean-Paul Sartre had no idea of meditation.

That is the misery of Western man. Western man is missing the flowering of life because he knows nothing about meditation, and Eastern man is missing because he knows nothing of love.

And to me, just as man and woman are halves of one whole; so are love and meditation.

Meditation is man; love is woman.

In the meeting of meditation and love is the meeting of man and woman. And in that meeting, we create the transcendental human being – which is neither man nor woman.

Unless we create the transcendental man on the earth, there is not much hope.

But I feel my people are capable of doing the apparently impossible.

Beloved Osho,

Even in my childhood I never rebelled when something wasn't authentic. I learned to wear a mask. I learned it so well that it is very difficult for me to see whether I'm authentic or phony.

Tomorrow I am going to take sannyas.

Is it alright with You to have a disciple who has so little authenticity and who hardly knows what love is?

The question is such ... it is as if you are sick and you go to a physician and ask him, "Is it alright for you to accept a sick man as a patient, or do you accept only the healthy people?"

My whole business is to accept all kinds of people – hypocrites with all kinds of masks ... insincere ... obedient against their own intelligence. But these are the people who need me, and these are the people I need too.

Bring all your sicknesses.

Don't be worried, I have even initiated a few dead people in the hope that resurrection is possible!

Beloved Osho,

Sometimes life seems to be such a drag that I would rather like to die. Any advice?

There are many methods to die, but one thing: anybody who really wants to die never asks for advice. Living may be a drag, but death is very quick. All around you, there are so many ways....

But you don't want to die.

In fact, even the people who commit suicide don't want to commit suicide. They commit suicide because they expected too much from life and they could not get it. The failure was so great, that to live shamefully became difficult. They committed suicide not *against* life; they committed suicide because they could not manage to learn the art of life. They wanted life to be a great benediction, and it was a drag.

It seems to be a fallacy all over the world that just because you are born you know how to live.

This is not right.

To be born is one thing. To know the art of living and of living fully is totally different.

Birth is only an opportunity – you can make it or mar it. Birth is not equivalent to life. Almost everybody thinks that birth is equivalent to life; so it is bound to become a drag – just breathing, eating every day, going to sleep, waking up in the morning, going to the same office, the same files and the same routine. For idiots it is perfectly okay, but for anybody who has some intelligence it is bound to become a drag. Because he can see – what is the point? Why after all am I living? If tomorrow is again going to be just a repetition of today, as today has been a repetition of yesterday, then why go on living? What is the point of unnecessarily repeating the same circle, the same routine, the same happenings?

But the fallacy is in the fact that you have accepted a wrong concept, that birth is life.

Birth is only an opportunity.

Either you can learn to live a beautiful life or you can just drag yourself towards the graveyard.

It is up to you. There are people for whom life is a drag, and there are people for whom even death is a dance.

I want to say to you that if you make your life an art, your death will be the culmination of the art – the highest peak, a beauty in itself.

Millions are there, who are in the same position as your question. They don't know why they are living and they don't know if there is any point in dying either. Life is futile – how can death appear to be significant? So they are afraid of suicide also, because if life is such – just a dark hole – death is going to be even worse.

One day I saw Nasruddin with his gun, a rope, and a tin of kerosene oil. I said, "Where are you going, Mulla?"

He said, "Enough is enough. I was just coming to say goodbye to you. I am going to commit suicide."

I said, "But so many arrangements?"

He said, "You know me, I am a perfectionist. I don't take chances. I have made every arrangement."

I said, "Can I come just to watch, and just to wave when you are disappearing in smoke?"

He said, "You can come."

So I went with him and sat on a rock by the side of a river. He made the arrangements very efficiently. On a branch of a tree which was hanging over the river, he tied the rope by which he was going to hang himself

I said, "Mulla, that's enough."

He said, "I don't believe it.... Unless I have done everything ... no loopholes should be left."

He put his neck into the rope, poured the kerosene oil over himself.

I said, "Mulla, is it going to be real?"

He said, "What do you think?"

He lit a match, set fire to himself, and before jumping from the tree, he fired the gun – the last resort – at his head.

But that's where everything went wrong – the gun missed the mark and cut the rope and he fell into the river ... naturally, the fire was finished, and he started swimming!

I said, "Mulla, what are you doing?"

He said, "What to do? I know how to swim."

I said, "This is strange. You arranged everything so well, but still there was a loophole, the swimming. You should not have started to swim. You should have remained there and died."

He said, "That's just it – dying is not so easy. When I saw the gun had misfired, when I saw the water had put the fire out, it became clear: God wants me to live. And moreover, I know how to swim! It is impossible when you know swimming not to swim. Next time, some other arrangement...."

Nobody wants to die.

And it is true that life is a drag.

But it is not *life* that is a drag, it is *you* – you have not learned the art of making life a joy, a thing of beauty, a piece of art.

Unless a man is creative, he cannot find much joy in life.

So the first principle is: Be creative.

Don't bother whether you become a world-famous artist or not; that is not the significant thing. But create something – a beautiful song, a little music, a dance, a painting, a garden. And when the roses blossom ... you cannot say that life is a drag with so many roses blossoming. A beautiful painting ... you cannot say life is a drag, because this painting has been created for the first time in the world and for the last time. Nobody has done it before, and nobody will do it again; only you were capable of doing it.

Express your uniqueness in whatsoever you do.

Express your individuality.

Let existence be proud of you.

Life will not be felt like a drag; it will become a fragrance.

Not only will life be a joy and a dance – for a creative person, for a meditative person, even death will be transformed.

I have always loved a story about Bokoju, a Zen master.

He was ninety years old when he died. Three days before, he informed all his disciples: "If you want to come for the last goodbye, then come. In three days' time I am going to leave the world."

So thousands of his disciples came – and he was one of the most unique masters Zen has produced. On the third day, in the morning there was a great gathering in his garden. He was lying under his most beautiful tree.

He suddenly asked, "Just tell me one thing: in what way should I die? – because I don't want to die like everybody else. Ninety-nine percent of people die in their beds." He said, "That is out of the question. Remove the bed from here!"

The bed is the most dangerous thing. Ninety-nine percent of people die there, and every night you go to bed without thinking of the danger. When the light is turned off, just put your mattress down on the floor. Then there is some chance of surviving – death may try to search for you on the bed and may not be able to find you.

Bokoju said, "Take this bed away from here, and suggest something, something unique, worthy of Bokoju."

The disciples thought – what to suggest? Somebody said that, "You can die sitting in a lotus posture. Many masters have died in the lotus posture."

But Bokoju said; "That is not very unique, because many people have died in that posture."

Somebody said, "You can die standing."

He said, "That seems to be appealing."

But one man objected; he said, "That's not right, because I know of a Zen master who died standing. It will not be unique."

Bokoju said, "It is very difficult. Find out quickly because my time is running out, and I cannot delay any more. So many idiots are here, and you cannot find just one unique way of dying for your beloved master?"

One man suggested, "Nobody has ever died standing on his head. You can do a headstand and die."

Bokoju said, "Perfectly right!"

He stood on his head and died.

Now the problem was.... The disciples said, "What to do?" – because they know what has to be done when a person dies in his bed. But what to do with this fellow who has died standing on his head?

Somebody said, "His elder sister, who is also a great master, lives just close by. It is better to call her and not to interfere, because this is a strange thing. We will be condemned later on if we don't do the right thing, so it is better to call somebody who can take responsibility."

The sister came and she said, "Bokoju! From your very childhood you have been mischievous – and this is no time to be mischievous! Just lie down!"

And Bokoju laughed and said, "Okay sister – because I cannot disobey you. I was almost dead. I was just waiting to see what these people would do trying to work out what to do with me after death. But these idiots have brought *you* here! And you always were a killjoy. You've destroyed the whole fun! Now I will die in the ordinary, orthodox way." And he died.

And his sister did not even look back, she just went away.

People said, "But he has died!"

She said, "It was time. He was delaying it. And it is not right to play jokes on existence. At least at the time of death one should be serious! Now he is dead, you do whatever you want to do. Even if he is not dead, finish him off – his time is up!"

Make your life....

Find out why you are feeling bored. Change.

It is such a small life.

Take risks, be a gambler – what can you lose?

We come with empty hands, we go with empty hands. There is nothing to lose.

Just a little time to be playful, to sing a beautiful song, and the time is gone.

Each moment is so precious.

If you are silent, if you are creative, if you are loving, if you are sensitive to beauty, if you are grateful to this vast universe...

There are millions of stars, which are dead – and you are so small, yet you have the most precious thing in existence ... life.

And not only life, but the possibility of becoming a consciousness, of becoming enlightened, of coming to a space where death has never entered.

If Bokoju is not serious, the reason is because he knows there is no death, it is only changing houses, or changing clothes at the most. It is excitement – even death is a great excitement and ecstasy.

It is just your wrong approach.

Drop it, and don't drop it slowly slowly, piece by piece.

Drop it totally, instantly.

When you go out of this place, go dancing and singing. Let the whole world think you are insane, that is far better.

Beloved Osho,

In 1980 You gave me sannyas. *I was not even looking for a master.
Since then I have experienced the joy and fun of being one of Your disciples.
But now I start feeling the pain: You are so vast — where is the way?
Is there a way?*

Just to be true is so difficult.

And is that all?

You have asked three questions in one question.

First, you found me although you were not looking for a master.
Let me make it clear to you that I was looking for a disciple, and
that is far more important.

Your looking for a master is not so important because you are asleep
and dreaming. So whenever I see some sleepwalker passing by, and see
some possibility that he can be awakened, I just turn his way — and he is
a sleepwalker so there is no problem. It does not matter where he is going.
I give him *sannyas*, he takes *sannyas* — because in sleep it does not matter.

I create a beautiful dream for him.

I am not a hard taskmaster. First I create a beautiful dream, and
then slowly slowly I take you out of it.

Now you are out of the dream, so the second problem arises – where is the path?

In fact, it is my doing. While you were asleep I was talking about the path ... "the path, the mystic path ..." to wake you up. Now you are awake so you are asking, "Where is the path?"

There is no path.

It was just a device to wake you up.

You are not to go anywhere. You are exactly at the place where you have to reach. You are exactly that which you have to become.

There is no path, there is no goal.

Your isness is your realization.

And thirdly: waking up, you see me vast like an ocean: While you were asleep, you were not aware of where I was leading you. Now you are fully awake, and you see the vast ocean.

It is not me. It is the reality – and it is *your* reality.

And the ocean that you are seeing outside you will remain outside you till your dewdrop disappears into it.

And the dewdrop is slipping from the lotus leaf. Any moment it will be part of the ocean and you will know that no man is an island; we all belong to one reality, one consciousness, one continent.

It is only in our sleep that we are separate.

The moment we are awake we are one.

There will be a little fear. It is said that even before a river falls into the ocean, it trembles with fear. It looks back at the whole journey, the peaks of the mountains, the long winding path through the forests, through the people, and it sees in front of it such a vast ocean that entering into it is nothing but disappearing forever. But there is no other way.

The river cannot go back.

Neither can you go back.

Going back is impossible in existence; you can only go forward. The river has to take the risk and go into the ocean.

And only when it enters the ocean will the fear disappear because only then will the river know that it is not disappearing into the ocean; rather it is becoming the ocean.

It is a disappearance from one side and it is a tremendous resurrection on the other side.

So don't be worried. Things are happening perfectly right for you.

You had not come in search of a master, but what to do? A master was in search of you.

And now there is no going back. Even if you try to close your eyes, that sleep in which you were living cannot be recalled.

And the vastness is not something to be afraid of. It is very friendly, it is very loving. Disappearing into it is almost like finding the womb and its warmth and its nourishment again.

Beloved Osho,

Do You have any problem which You have not solved yet?

I don't have any problem. I used to have problems, but I never solved them. My procedure is totally different. I *dissolve* the problem; I never solve it – because solving does not help. You solve a problem, and you will find that ten other problems have arisen out of your solution.

I have been dissolving, I have been *getting rid* of – because no problem is significant. All problems are barriers between you and existence.

Now I have only mysteries – no problems, no questions.

In that way I am a very poor man.

No problem, no question; I am utterly silent. But silence has a richness that millions of problems cannot give to you. Silence has a richness that all the philosophies of the world and all the answers together cannot give you.

When I answer your questions, it is not that I have got an answer and I simply give it to you. I don't have any answer.

I simply listen to your question and let my silence respond to it; hence, you can find many contradictions in my answers. But I am not responsible, because I have never answered.

It is the silence that goes on responding at different moments in different times to different people in different ways. Just as you listen to the answer, I also listen to it.

There is no speaker here.

Here, there are only listeners.

Beloved Osho,

What is the last question we should ask You, Osho?

There is not even a first question, so the question about the last question does not arise.

You should learn to be silent, to be at ease with me, to be in tune with me. In that silent harmony all is achieved: all the treasures that existence has been keeping safe for you, so that when you wake up you can claim your portion.

And everybody's portion of the treasure is infinite. It is not that because it is a portion, it will be limited.

The *upanishadic* seers have said: You can take out even the whole from the whole, yet the whole remains behind.

Existence is such a mystery that it can give to each person infinite treasure, eternal life, unbounded beauty.

So don't be worried about the last question. There is not even a first question.

Be innocent and silent, and just be open and receptive to my heartbeats. The moment your heartbeats are also dancing to the same tune, you have come home.

In fact, you have never gone anywhere. You have just forgotten that this is your home.

5

THE POINT OF NO RETURN

Beloved Osho,

Sri Aurobindo declared that there is something beyond that which Buddha calls enlightenment. His whole aspiration was dedicated towards opening a door for this new step in human evolution.

Beloved Osho, what could not happen with Aurobindo, is it happening with You?

S ri Aurobindo is a strange case. He knows everything about enlightenment, but he is not enlightened.

He is one of the greatest scholars of this age, a genius; vast is his knowledge. But his knowing is nil. He knows about the scriptures, and he knows better than anybody else. His interpretation is profound, very logical, but heartless. It is dead; it is not coming out of his own realization.

This is one of the great problems for all seekers of truth: one can get lost in knowledge without knowing anything about the reality. He knows all the theories, all the philosophies, but he is just a blind man who knows but has not seen the light himself. And it is possible to remain in a deception for your whole life – because you know so much, and people start worshipping you, people start believing you. And belief has its own psychology: if many people believe in you, you are bound to believe in yourself.

I have often told a small story about a great journalist who died and reached the doors of heaven.

The doors of heaven and hell are not far apart; they are just opposite each other. The distance is not much, and naturally one would like to enter heaven. So he knocked on the door. The doorkeeper opened a small window in the door and asked, "What do you want?"

He said, "I am a great journalist. I have just died, and I want to enter."

The doorkeeper said, "I am sorry but I have to refuse you because we have a quota; we can have only twelve journalists in heaven. That quota has been filled for centuries – for centuries, no new journalist has entered. And anyway, even those twelve are utterly useless because nothing happens in heaven. They tried to publish a newspaper, but only one issue appeared – because there are only saints here – no murder, no suicide, no crime, no politics, no struggle for power ... no change ever happens; everything is eternally the same. From where can you get news?"

"And," the doorkeeper said, "you must have heard the definition of news: when a dog bites a man it is not news, but when a man bites a dog it is news. So nothing sensational happens here, no love affair... When people get bored, they read the first issue that was published centuries ago.

"You should go to hell. Every moment tremendous things happen there. All the active people of the world, all the creative people of the world are there – painters, musicians, poets, actors, dancers, thieves, murderers, rapists, psychoanalysts, philosophers – you will find every variety.

"Heaven is monotonous. Only dull, dead saints – skeletons. Their only quality is that they don't do anything. So just go to hell and enjoy. You will find everything that you may have missed on earth – because for centuries upon centuries, all the juicy people have collected there. In fact, I myself want to go ... but once you get into heaven, you cannot escape. So I am stuck here. My suggestion is that you just go."

But journalists are stubborn people. He said, "I have a suggestion, and I think you must be compassionate enough to do it for me. Just give me twenty-four hours' entry. If I can convince one of the journalists inside to go to hell then you can put me in the quota; twelve journalists will remain twelve."

The gatekeeper said, "It is unheard of, there is no precedent. But I cannot say no to you. Go in, have a try. But remember, after twenty-four hours.... I am taking a risk. After twenty-four hours, come back."

After twenty-four hours he came back. In those twenty-four hours he had created a rumor among all the journalists: "A big newspaper is going to be started in hell and there is great need for editors, sub-editors, story writers, all kinds of journalists. The salaries are great. So what are you doing here?"

After twenty-four hours the journalist came back. The gatekeeper said, "Go back. You can't go out now."

The journalist said, "Why not?"

The gatekeeper said, "I have kept my word, and you have to keep your word. You were very convincing. All twelve journalists have gone: I tried hard to explain that 'This is just a rumor; don't spoil your heaven.' But they wouldn't listen."

The man himself had created the rumor, but he had started thinking perhaps there was something in it; otherwise twelve persons wouldn't go to hell for no reason.

He said, "Just open the door!" He was convinced by others being convinced.

And this happens to millions of people.

When you see that seven hundred million people are convinced that Catholic Christianity is the only religion, it is difficult to say that those seven hundred million people can be wrong. The sheer number has such weight.

That's why all the religions go on trying to increase their numbers. They have their methods to increase their numbers because the more you increase the numbers the more you convince those who are not in your fold that they are wrong and you are right. Your sheer majority is an argument; it validates anything you say.

Sri Aurobindo was a great intellectual, a very convincing, rational philosophical genius. He convinced many people, and those many people convinced him that he was enlightened.

He knows nothing of enlightenment. It is true that there is something more in existence than the enlightenment Gautam the Buddha achieved. But it is Gautam the Buddha himself who, for the first time in the world, indicated the possibility of the beyond. Naturally, nobody else can say that there is something beyond – unless they reach that boundary.

So when Sri Aurobindo says there is something more than the enlightenment of Gautam Buddha, he is hiding the fact that it was Gautam Buddha himself who was the first man in the whole of history to say that "This is not all; there is something beyond."

Buddha says – and you can see the sincerity of the man – that "A man who has entered the path, *srotapanna*, who has entered the stream that leads to the ocean, is millions of times more respectable than anybody else, just because he has entered the path in search of the truth. He has not found, but just the urge, just the effort, the first step, and he has become millions of times more honorable than all your respectable generals, kings, emperors and world conquerors.

"The person who has reached the point from which he will not turn back, *anagamin*, is millions of times more honorable than the *srotapanna*, than the one who has entered the stream. And the man who has become enlightened, who has become a *buddha*, is millions of times more honorable than the person who has reached the point of no return."

The point of no return is something worth understanding.

Many people start the search and then drop out. It is arduous, it is moving into the unknown; nobody knows whether there is anything like enlightenment or just a fiction created by a few people like Gautam Buddha. Perhaps they are not lying, perhaps they themselves are deceived – who knows?

There is no guarantee.

So many start, but very few remain. Most of them return to the world. Sooner or later, finding that they are going into an unknown territory without a map, without any guide, they start feeling crazy. Because the whole world is going in a totally different direction, and they are left alone. Their whole strength was in the crowd. Alone, a thousand and one doubts arise. Alone, one starts feeling that millions of people cannot be wrong, "And I am alone, thinking that I am right – I must be getting crazy."

Anagamin is one who has come to a point from where he cannot return. He is not enlightened but he has seen, from far away, the possibility. He has not reached the peak; he is still in the dark valley. But he can see the sunlit peak; it is a reality, it is not a fiction. Now there is no force in the world which can make him go back.

Buddha says, "But the one who has become enlightened is millions of times more honorable than the person who has reached the point of no return."

And here is the sincerity of the man – he says: "The man who has transcended *buddhahood*, who has gone beyond enlightenment, is millions of times more honorable than anyone who is enlightened." He is not claiming that he has gone beyond; he is simply saying "I can see from my place that faraway star."

And he was the first to see that faraway star: beyond enlightenment.

Sri Aurobindo is not sincere. He never quotes this passage, which was his duty to quote. He tries to convince his readers and followers that he is working to open the door beyond enlightenment. He is not even courageous enough to declare himself ... to say that he is enlightened. He never declared that. But only indirectly ... he is assuming that you will understand that he is enlightened because he is trying to open the door beyond enlightenment. Naturally he must be enlightened, but he is not saying it.

To declare it needs courage, not scholarship.

He gives a hint, as if he is enlightened and he is working for others so that they can also go beyond enlightenment. They have not even reached enlightenment. It is hilarious, the very idea that he is trying to open the door ... his whole life's aspiration.

All his aspirations were stupid.

This is stupid because others will need that door only if they have become enlightened. First help people to become enlightened! Rather than helping people to become enlightened, you are devoting your whole energy to opening the door beyond enlightenment.

And it is not only on this point that he was talking nonsense, he was talking nonsense on many points.

Another of his aspirations was physical immortality; he was working so that man can become physically immortal. Naturally you will think *he* has become physically immortal – these are natural assumptions. And his followers all over the world started spreading the great news, the good news, that Sri Aurobindo had become physically immortal: "Now he is trying to find the right techniques so that every human being can become physically immortal." And then one day he died.

One of my friends was living in Sri Aurobindo's *ashram*. I phoned him immediately and asked him, "What happened?"

But such is blindness ... he said, "Here in the *ashram* everybody was shocked. But the mother of the *ashram* told us that he has simply gone into a long *samadhi*. He is not dead; it is part of his project to find immortality. He has found all, but just for the last, missing link he has to go into deep *samadhi*, to dive deep into the ocean." And he told me that everybody believed it!

For three days they did not cremate his body or bury his body because they believed that he would be coming back. But in three days the body started stinking. Then they became afraid that if the news spread that the body was stinking....

The man was dead, he was not going to come back. After three days they put his body into a marble grave.

Still they did not burn his body because he might come back at any moment. The really faithful ones still believe that one day he will come back. And the whole belief shifted towards the mother – she was the co-partner in the business of finding immortality for humanity. And it looked as if she *had* found it, because she lived for almost a century. It seemed probable; perhaps she had found it. And she was saying that she was going to live forever.

Now this is the beautiful thing about spirituality: I can say to you that I am going to live forever and tomorrow I can die – who are you going to argue with?

And one day the mother died. Again the same thing: they waited for three days, and when the body started stinking, she was put into another marble grave next to Sri Aurobindo. And the faithful ones still sit beside the graves every day, waiting for them to return. Slowly slowly, the number of faithful ones is lessening. The hope is turning into hopelessness, into despair. Perhaps they have not yet found the missing link together.

It is enough that man has an immortal soul, an immortal consciousness, an immortal life principle.

But Sri Aurobindo was obsessed with the idea that he had to bring some original contribution to the spiritual progress of humanity. That the human soul is immortal is as ancient an experience as humanity itself. Even the *Vedas,* five thousand years old, declare man as *amritasya putrah* – "you are sons of immortality." Something new, something original ... and this was a great original idea, that your body can be immortal.

One cannot conceive how intelligent people can get caught up in such absurd ideas.

Sri Aurobindo was a child, he became a young man, he became old. If the human body is immortal, then you will have to say at what age it is going to be immortal. As a child? As a young man? As an old man? Or as a dead man? The last seems to be the only possibility.

"As a dead man, the human body is immortal" – and certainly it is, because all the elements of the human body disperse into nature. Nothing is going to die, everything is going to merge – the earth into earth, the water into water, the air into air ... all the elements will go to their sources. In that sense the human body has always been immortal. Not only the human body – buffaloes, donkeys, monkeys, *everybody* is immortal. It does not need a Sri Aurobindo to declare that his body is immortal.

Gautam Buddha is the rarest human being in that he recognizes that there is still something more, he has not reached the end of evolution.

In Japan, they had a beautiful collection of paintings called "Ten Zen Bulls." It is a series of paintings depicting the whole story of the search.

In the first, a man is looking here and there ... his bull is lost. You see forest all around, ancient trees, and the puzzled man standing there looking, and he cannot see the bull.

In the second painting, he looks a little happier because he has seen the bull's footprints. It is the same painting, the same forest. Just one thing he has discovered in this painting and that is, he has seen the bull's footprints, so he knows where he has gone.

In the third painting he moves and sees the backside of the bull because it is standing by the side of a tree, and the man is behind him – so he looks ... and just the backside is shown in the painting.

In the fourth he has reached the bull; he sees the whole bull.

In the fifth he has caught hold of the bull by the horns.

In the sixth he is riding on the bull. It is difficult, the bull is trying to throw him off.

By the eighth he is returning home, the bull is conquered.

In the ninth the bull is back in the stall and the man is playing on a flute.

In the tenth, there is no question of the bull at all. The man is seen in the marketplace with a bottle of wine, drunk.

Buddhists were very much embarrassed about the tenth painting. It does not seem to be Buddhist at all – and there is no connection, because nine seems to be perfect; there is no need for the tenth.

So in the Middle Ages they dropped the tenth painting, and they started talking of the nine paintings. Only recently has the tenth painting been discovered again in the ancient scriptures with its description – because each painting has a description of what is happening. The bull is lost, your soul is lost – the bull represents your soul, your energy, your spirit. When the bull is found, you have become a realized soul. You are singing a song on the flute – that is the stage of enlightenment.

What about the tenth? That is the stage when you go beyond enlightenment; you become ordinary again. Now there is no split between this world and that, now there is no split between good and bad. Now all opposites have joined together into one single harmony; that's what is represented by the bottle of wine, a bottle of wine in the hands of a *buddha*.

Sri Aurobindo never talked about the Ten Bulls because again it would have destroyed his originality. The paintings of the Ten Bulls are at least fifteen centuries old.

The Buddhists in the Middle Ages were cowardly; they could not understand the tenth.

But as far as I am concerned, I can see a natural growth from the ninth to the tenth, from enlightenment to beyond enlightenment.

Enlightenment makes you special. That means something of the ego in some subtle form still remains. Others are ignorant, you are a knower; others are going towards hell, your paradise is guaranteed. These are the last remnants of a dying ego. And when this ego also dies the *buddha* becomes an ordinary human being not knowing at all that he is holier than thou, higher than thou, special in any sense – so ordinary that even a bottle of wine is acceptable. The whole of life is acceptable; the days and the nights, the flowers and the thorns, the saints and the sinners – all are acceptable, with no discrimination at all.

This ordinariness is really the greatest flowering of human reality.

Sri Aurobindo will be remembered as a great philosopher – *should* be remembered as a great philosopher – a man of tremendous insight into words, scriptures; immensely articulate in bringing meanings, interpretations to them; novel, original... But he was not a man of realization. And he is not sincere, he is not an authentic man.

He had a great desire to prove himself, to prove that he is greater than Gautam Buddha. That was his ego.

To go beyond enlightenment is not to become greater than Gautam Buddha.

To go beyond enlightenment is to become an ordinary human being. To forget all about enlightenment and all about great spiritual aspirations and to live simply joyously, playfully ... this ordinariness is the most extraordinary phenomenon in the world.

But you will not be able to recognize him. Up to Gautam Buddha you will be able to recognize, but as a person moves beyond Gautam Buddha, he will start slipping out of your hands.

Those who have recognized him as an enlightened being may remain aware of who he is, but those who come new will not be able to recognize him at all, because he will be simply a very innocent, ordinary, human being – just like a child collecting seashells on the beach, running after butterflies, gathering flowers. No division of body and soul, no division of matter and spirit, no division of this life and that – all that is forgotten; one has relaxed totally.

If Sri Aurobindo had known even the meaning of what it is to go beyond realization, beyond enlightenment, he would not have even thought about it. He was thinking that going beyond enlightenment is something greater than Gautam Buddha. He was continuously in an inner jealousy, and of course the jealousy was of Gautam Buddha.

And he wanted to come up with some original ideas so that he could prove them, but he has not proved anything.

I respect Sri Aurobindo as a scholar – but scholars are just scholars, a dollar a dozen.

Beloved Osho,

The other night You talked about the master and the mystic. My question is about the mystic and the skeptic.

Is it possible for a skeptic to become a mystic?

So much of the esoteric and mystical seems to be a process of autosuggestion, imagination and wishful thinking. I sometimes feel very discouraged and want to give it all up as nonsense. Yet there is also an inner voice leading me on. The biggest relief for me seems to be in Your continual encouragement to let go and trust.

Beloved Master, do You see any possibility for a skeptic to get through this conglomeration of mind fabrications?

The skeptical mind is one of the most beautiful things in the world. It has been condemned by the religions because they were not capable of answering skeptical questions; they wanted only believers.

And the skeptical mind is just the opposite of the believer.

I am all in favor of the skeptical mind. Do not believe anything unless you have experienced it. Do not believe anything – go on questioning, however long it takes.

Truth is not cheap. It is not available to the believer; it is available only to the skeptical.

Just remember one thing: don't be skeptical half-heartedly. Be a *total* skeptic.

When I say be a total skeptic, I mean that your skeptical ideas should also be put to the same test as anybody else's beliefs. Skepticism, when it is total, burns itself out because you have to question and doubt your skepticism too.

You cannot leave your skepticism without doubt; otherwise that is the standpoint of the believer.

If you can doubt the skeptic in you, then the mystic is not far away.

What is a mystic? – one who knows no answer, one who has asked every possible question and found that no question is answerable. Finding this, he has dropped questioning. Not that he has found the answer – he has simply found one thing, that there is no answer anywhere.

Life is a mystery, not a question. Not a puzzle to be solved, not a question to be answered but a mystery to be lived, a mystery to be loved, a mystery to be danced.

A totally skeptical mind is bound to finally become a mystic; hence, my doors are open for all. I accept the skeptic because I know how to turn him into a mystic. I invite the theist because I know how to destroy his theism. I invite the atheist because I know how to take away his atheism. My doors prevent nobody, because I am not giving you any belief. I am giving you only a methodology, a meditation to discover for yourself what in reality is the case.

I have found that there is no answer. All questions are futile, and all answers are more futile. Questions have been asked by foolish people, and great philosophies have arisen because of their questions. These philosophies are created by the cunning and the shrewd.

But if you want to have a rapport with reality, you have to be neither a fool nor shrewd. You have to be innocent. So whatever you bring – skepticism, atheism, theism, communism, fascism, any type of nonsense you can bring here – my medicine is the same.

It does not matter what kind of nonsense is filled in your head when you come here. I will chop your head without any distinction. Who is sitting on your head does not matter – my concern is chopping!

I am just a woodcutter.

Beloved Osho,

I cannot find the question, but my heart needs an answer. What is it?

It is a very profound inquiry.
Anybody who is sincere will have the same inquiry.

All questions are foolish, silly at the most. But still there is some existential need for an answer.

The question is not known.

I have told you about one of the most beautiful woman poets, Gertrude Stein. She was dying, and a small circle of friends had gathered around her. Just before her death she opened her eyes and asked, "What is the answer?"

They were all puzzled because this is not the way ... first you have to ask the question. She is first asking what the answer is – answer to what? But you cannot be hard to a dying woman – and no ordinary woman, a really great poet. And even in this statement her greatness is absolutely present.

For a few seconds there was silence. Then one person gathered courage and said, "Stein, you have not asked the question. This is strange that you are asking what the answer is."

So the dying woman opened her eyes and said, "Okay. So tell me what the question is." And she died.

This is something truly mystic.

There is no question, but there is an existential thirst which appears to the mind as a search for an answer. But there is no answer.

Existence is, and it is tremendously beautiful, psychedelically colorful. It is song and dance and celebration all over.

But please don't ask any question or any answer.

It is a mystery. Mystery means there is no way to solve it, whatever you do is going to fail. Rather, live it – drop solving. Perhaps through living you will come to an understanding. But that will not be the answer, it will be *more* than the answer; it will be an alive experience. You will have become part of the mystery itself.

Even the greatest philosophers have been behaving like children. They go on representing life as if it is a puzzle, a crossword puzzle.

It is not a puzzle. It is simply an unanswerable but experienceable phenomenon.

That's what I mean by 'mysticism'.

Philosophers miss it completely because they try to find questions, and then answers.

Questions are man-made.

A rosebush never asks a question, a cloud never bothers about a question, a mountain never raises a question. It does not mean that they have the answer; is simply means they are beyond the question-answer game.

And when I say 'going beyond enlightenment' I am saying the same thing in other words – going beyond the question-answer game and just accepting reality as it is, whatsoever it is.

Otherwise, there are troubles upon troubles. First you create the question, then you create the answer. Then the answer creates ten more questions; you create ten more answers and then each answer creates ten more questions. It is like a tree; it goes on growing and becoming bigger and bigger and there is no end.

Just live your life simply, without putting a question mark behind every experience. People may think you are crazy, but if *you* are crazy then the whole of existence is crazy – what to do? It is out of our hands.

Why does the sun rise in the morning every day? Not even a single day is a holiday. Not even for a single day does it rise from the West – just for a change: "I am getting tired of rising from the East...."

No, things are simply going so smoothly ... just man is in trouble.

The moment you also start living like a rosebush, rising like a sun, floating like a white cloud, you have come to a profound understanding of the mysterious, of the miraculous truth of existence.

Beloved Osho,

A woman friend of mine often uses the words "male ego" about me, which I feel is not true about me.

From the very beginning I have been open and vulnerable to feminine energy, which is teaching me to become a disciple every day. Moreover, I have felt that when she used this word there was some kind of hatred towards men.

Osho, can You explain what the "male ego" is, and what it means when a woman uses this expression about a man?

The ego is simply the ego, it is neither male nor female.

But man has been very inhuman towards women for centuries, continuously. And the strange thing is that the man has been so cruel and inhuman towards women because he feels a deep inferiority complex in comparison to them.

The greatest problem has been that the woman is capable of becoming a mother; she is capable of giving birth to life, and man is not. That was the beginning of the feeling of inferiority – that nature depends on woman, not on man.

Moreover, he has found that she is in many ways stronger than him.

For example, for every one hundred and fifteen boys that are born, only one hundred girls are born – because fifteen boys will pop off by the time they become sexually mature, but the girls will remain; they have a certain stamina. Women fall sick less than men. Women commit suicide less than men – although they talk about suicide more, they simply talk. At the most they take sleeping pills, but always in such a small quantity that they never die. Men commit suicide in almost double the numbers. Women live five years longer than men.

Women are more patient, more tolerant than men. Men are very impatient and very intolerant. Women are less violent than men. Women don't commit murders; it is the man who commits murders, who wages crusades, who is always getting ready for war, who invents all kinds of deadly weapons – atomic bombs, nuclear weapons.

The woman is completely out of this whole game of death.

Hence it was no coincidence that man started feeling somehow inferior. And nobody wants to be inferior; the only way was to force the woman in artificial ways to become inferior. For example, not to allow her education, not to allow her economic freedom, not to allow her to move out of the house, but confine her to an imprisonment.

It seems almost unbelievable what man has done to woman just to get rid of his inferiority. He has made the woman artificially inferior.

In China, for five thousand years it was thought that women had no soul. Of course all the writers were men; they proposed the idea that a woman is only a machine, a reproductive machine. And the idea gained so much influence that it even entered the justice system of China. If a man murdered his wife, he was not a criminal – because he had simply broken a chair, a table ... at the most a television. But it was *his* property, and he had the right to destroy it.

So in China, thousands of women were killed by their husbands. But the husbands could not be punished by the government or the courts, because the basic principle that the woman had a soul was denied.

In India for ten thousand years the woman was told that even to dream of some other man is a sin. The same was not said to the man. The woman had to live a very virtuous life while for the man there was freedom. Man created prostitutes for his freedom.

And this possessiveness in India took on almost insane proportions. When a man died, his wife had to die with him.. She had to jump alive into the funeral pyre – and for ten thousand years that continued. If some woman was afraid – anybody would be afraid to jump alive into a funeral pyre – then she was condemned as immoral.

The husband's wish was that she should die with him because he could not trust her – when he is gone, she may start having some love affair with somebody else, and this cannot be tolerated.

But the strange thing is that the same rule was not applicable to men, that when the wife dies the husband should jump into the funeral pyre. No, man was a higher quality of being.

The way they used to do it brings tears ... because to burn a woman alive is not an easy task. First they would make the funeral pyre, put the dead body of the husband on it, force the woman to lie down next to the dead body. Then they would put more wood on top of both of them and pour refined butter all over the funeral pyre, so that the fire would get going fast, strong – and not *only* fast and strong, but it would create so much smoke that nobody could see what was happening there, because sometimes the woman would try to jump out of the funeral pyre.

There were priests standing around the funeral pyre with burning torches in their hands. If the woman tried to jump out, they would force her, with the burning torches, back into the funeral pyre.

Hence so much smoke was needed, so nobody could see what the priest was doing.

The woman was bound to cry and scream. Her screams should not be heard, so there was an arrangement: behind the priests, there was another row of thousands of people playing music, dancing, singing, shouting as loudly as possible just to drown out the screams of the woman coming from the funeral pyre. And they were celebrating, because one woman had proved her love, her trust by committing suicide.

She was forced; she did not come to do it willingly, she was brought there.

And the same situation has happened all over the world. In different ways, they have been cutting woman's wings, her abilities, her talents, her genius.

It is not only a question for you. When your woman is telling you that you have a male ego, she is simply representing all women, and you are nothing but a representative of all men. Your forefathers have done so much harm that there is no way to come to a balance.

So when your woman says that this is male ego, try to understand – perhaps she is right. Most probably she is right – because the male has accepted himself as superior for so long that he does not feel that it is his ego. It is the woman who feels it.

Don't deny her feeling. Be grateful to her, and ask her where she feels the ego so that you can drop it. Take her help.

You are simply denying it; you don't feel that you have any male ego. But it is simply a traditional heritage.

The Point of No Return ——————————————————————————●

Every small boy has a male ego – just a small boy, if he starts crying you immediately say, "Why are you crying like a girl? A girl is allowed to cry because she is subhuman. You are going to be a big male chauvinist; you are not supposed to cry or weep." And small boys start stopping their tears. It is very rare to find men who are as ready to cry and allow tears to flow as women are.

Remember, you both have the same size tear glands in your eyes, so nature does not make any difference. Listen to the woman. You have suppressed the woman and oppressed the woman so much, it is time that she should be listened to and things should be corrected. At least in your personal life do as much as you can to allow the woman as much freedom as possible – the same freedom that you allow yourself. Help her to stand up so that she can blossom again.

We will have a more beautiful world if all women – and women are half of the world – are allowed to grow their talents, their genius. It is not a question at all ... nobody is higher, nobody is lower. Women are women, men are men; they have differences, but differences don't make anybody higher or lower. Their differences create their attraction.

Just think of a world where there are only men. It will be so ugly, everywhere Morarji Desai ... Morarji Desai ... all drinking their urine, nothing else to do.

●——————————————————————————— 161

Life is rich because there are differences, different attitudes, different opinions. Nobody is superior, nobody is inferior. People are simply different.

Accept this, and help your woman to be free from ten thousand years of repression. Be a friend to her. Much harm has been done; she has been wounded so much that if you can do some healing with your love, you will be contributing to the whole world, to the whole world consciousness.

Don't feel bad if your woman says "this is male ego." It is there in a subtle form, unrecognizable because it has been there for so long; you have forgotten that this is ego. Take her help so that you can recognize it and destroy it.

•••

MEDITATION – THE COURAGE TO BE SILENT AND ALONE

MEDITATION – THE COURAGE
TO BE SILENT AND ALONE

Beloved Osho,

I am always afraid of being alone, because when I am alone I start to wonder who I am. It feels that if I inquire deeper, I will find out that I am not the person who I have believed I was for the past twenty-six years, but a being, present at the moment of birth and maybe also the moment before. For some reason, this scares me completely. It feels like a kind of insanity, and makes me lose myself in outside things in order to feel safer.

Osho, who am I, and why the fear?

S urabhi, it is not only your fear, it is everybody's fear. Because nobody is what he was supposed to be by existence.

The society, the culture, the religion, the education have all been conspiring against innocent children.

They have all the powers – the child is helpless and dependent. So whatsoever they want to make out of him, they manage to do it.

They don't allow any child to grow to his natural destiny.

Their every effort is to make human beings into utilities. Who knows, if a child is left on his own to grow, whether he will be of any use to the vested interests or not? The society is not prepared to take the risk. It grabs the child and starts molding him into something that is needed by the society.

In a certain sense, it kills the soul of the child and gives him a false identity, so that he never misses his soul, his being.

The false identity is a substitute. But that substitute is useful only in the same crowd which has given it to you. The moment you are alone, the false starts falling apart and the repressed real starts expressing itself.

Hence the fear of being lonely.

Nobody wants to be lonely. Everybody wants to belong to a crowd—not only one crowd, but many crowds. A person belongs to a religious crowd, a political party, a rotary club ... and there are many other small groups to belong to.

One wants to be supported twenty-four hours a day because the false without support, cannot stand. The moment one is alone, one starts feeling a strange craziness.

Surabhi, that's what you have been asking about – because for twenty-six years you believed yourself to be somebody, and then suddenly in a moment of loneliness you start feeling you are *not* that. It creates fear: then who are you?

And twenty-six years of suppression ... it will take some time for the real to express itself.

The gap between the two has been called by the mystics "the dark night of the soul" – a very appropriate expression. You are no more the false, and you are not yet the real. You are in a limbo, you don't know who you are.

Particularly in the West – and Surabhi comes from the West – the problem is even more complicated. Because they have not developed any methodology to discover the real as soon as possible, so that the dark night of the soul can be shortened.

The West knows nothing as far as meditation is concerned.

And meditation is only a name for being alone, silent, waiting for the real to assert itself. It is not an act, it is a silent relaxation – because whatever you *do* will come out of your false personality. All your doing for twenty-six years has come out of it; it is an old habit.

Habits die hard.

There was one great mystic in India, Eknath. He was going for a holy pilgrimage with all his disciples – it was almost three to six months' journey.

One man came to him, fell at his feet and said, "I know I am not worthy. You know it too, everybody knows me. But I know your compassion is greater than my unworthiness. Please accept me also as one of the members of the group that is going on the holy pilgrimage."

Eknath said, "You are a thief – and not an ordinary thief, but a master thief. You have never been caught, and everybody knows that you are a thief. I certainly feel like taking you with me, but I also have to think about those fifty people who are going with me. You will have to give me a promise – and I am not asking for more, just for these three

———————● ——————————————— 167

ro six months' time while we are on the pilgrimage: you will not steal. After that, it is up to you. Once we are back home, you are free from the promise."

The man said, "I am absolutely ready to promise, and I am tremendously grateful for your compassion." The other fifty people were suspicious. To trust in a thief....

But they could not say anything to Eknath. He was the master.

The pilgrimage started, and from the very first night there was trouble. The next morning there was chaos – somebody's coat was missing, somebody's shirt was missing, somebody's money was gone.

And everybody was shouting, "Where is my money?" and they were all telling Eknath, "We were suspicious from the very beginning that you were taking this man with you. A lifelong habit...."

But then they started looking, and they found that things were not stolen. Somebody's money was missing, but it was found in somebody else's bag. Somebody else's coat was missing, but it was found in somebody else's luggage. Everything was found, but it was an unnecessary trouble – every morning!

And nobody could conceive – what can be the meaning of it? And now certainly it is not the thief, because nothing is stolen.

The third night, Eknath remained awake to see what goes on. In the middle of the night, the thief – just out of habit – woke up, started taking things from one place to another place. Eknath stopped him and said, "What are you doing? Have you forgotten your promise?"

He said, "No, I have not forgotten my promise. I am not stealing anything, but I have not promised that I will not change things from one place to another place. After six months I have to be a thief again; this is just practice. And you must understand it is a lifelong habit, you cannot drop it just like that. Just give me time. You should understand my problem also. For three days I have not stolen a single thing – it is just like fasting! This is just a substitute, I am keeping myself busy.

"This is my business time, in the middle of the night, so it is very hard for me just to lie down on the bed awake. And so many idiots are sleeping ... and I am not doing any harm to anybody. In the morning they will find their things."

Eknath said, "You are a strange man. You see that every morning there is such chaos, and one or two hours unnecessarily are wasted in finding things – where you have put them, whose thing has gone into whose luggage. Everybody has to open everything and ask everybody ... 'To whom does this belong?' "

The thief said, "This much concession you have to give to me."

Surabhi, twenty-six years of a false personality imposed by people who you loved, who you respected ... and they were not intentionally doing anything bad to you. Their intentions were good, just their awareness was nil. They were not conscious people – your parents, your teachers, your priests, your politicians – they were not conscious people, they were unconscious.

And even a good intention in the hands of an unconscious person turns out to be poisonous.

So whenever you are alone, a deep fear – because suddenly the false starts disappearing.

And the real will take a little time. You have lost it twenty-six years back. You will have to give some consideration to the fact that twenty-six years' gap has to be bridged.

In fear – that "I am losing myself, my senses, my sanity, my mind – everything" because the self that has been given to you by others consists of all these things – it looks like you will go insane: You immediately start doing something just to keep yourself engaged. If there are no people, at least there is some action. So the false remains engaged and does not start disappearing.

Hence people find it the most difficult on holidays. For five days they work, hoping that on the weekend they are going to relax. But the weekend is the worst time in the whole world – more accidents happen on the weekend, more people commit suicide, more murders, more stealing, more rape. Strange ... and these people were engaged for five days and there was no problem. But the weekend suddenly gives them a choice, either to be engaged in something or to relax – but relaxing is fearsome; the false personality disappears.

Keep engaged, do anything stupid. People are running towards the beaches, bumper to bumper, miles-long traffic. And if you ask them where they are going, they are getting away from the crowd – and the whole crowd is going with them. They are going to find a solitary, silent space – all of them.

In fact, if they had remained home it would have been more solitary and silent – because all the idiots have gone in search of a solitary place. And they are rushing like mad, because two days will be finished soon, they have to reach – don't ask where!

And on the beaches, you see ... they are so crowded, not even marketplaces are so crowded. And strangely enough, people are feeling very much at ease, taking a sunbath. Ten thousand people on a small beach taking a sunbath, relaxing.

The person on the same beach alone will not be able to relax. But he knows thousands of other people are relaxing all around him. The same people were in the offices, the same people were in the streets, the same people were in the marketplace, now the same people are on the beach.

The crowd is an essential for the false self to exist.

The moment it is lonely, you start freaking out.

This is where one should understand a little bit of meditation.

Don't be worried, because that which can disappear is worth disappearing. It is meaningless to cling to it – it is not yours, it is not you.

You are the one when the false has gone and the fresh, the innocent, the unpolluted being will arise in its place.

Nobody else can answer your question "Who am I?" – you will know it.

All meditative techniques are a help to destroy the false. They don't give you the real – the real cannot be given.

That which can be given cannot be real.

The real you have got already; just the false has to be taken away.

In a different way it can be said: the master takes away things from you which you don't really have, and he gives you that which you really have.

Meditation is just a courage to be silent and alone.

Slowly slowly, you start feeling a new quality to yourself, a new aliveness, a new beauty, a new intelligence – which is not borrowed from anybody, which is growing within you. It has roots in your existence.

And if you are not a coward, it will come to fruition, to flowering.

Only the brave, the courageous, the people who have guts, can be religious. Not the churchgoers – these are the cowards. Not the Hindus, not the Mohammedans, not the Christians – they are against searching. The same crowd, they are trying to make their false identity more consolidated.

You were born. You have come into the world with life, with consciousness, with tremendous sensitivity. Just look at a small child – look at his eyes, the freshness. All that has been covered by a false personality. There is no need to be afraid.

You can lose only that which *has* to be lost. And it is good to lose it soon – because the longer it stays, the stronger it becomes.

And one does not know anything about tomorrow.

Don't die before realizing your authentic being.

Only those few people are fortunate who have lived with authentic being and who have died with authentic being – because they know that life is eternal, and death is a fiction.

Beloved Osho,

Is sitting silently, doing nothing, watching the grass grow — and maybe falling asleep — really enough?

I once heard You say about Freud that he probably was not able to create himself. Or I heard You say that we create our own lives, our own hells and miseries, and that we are responsible.

If sitting silently really is enough, where does the word 'effort' or 'discipline' come in? Then, if we are doing something, what are we 'doing'? Can we do anything at all, or am I dreaming that I am doing something?

Somewhere I am so tired of it. But then also am I going to end up in a state of lethargy and indifference, in which I cannot see any love or beauty?

The people who have been exploiting humanity have created great philosophies, theologies, disciplines. Without the support of all this philosophical, theological, religious framework, it would be impossible to create the false personality.

The word 'discipline' comes from these people, and the word 'effort' also comes from these people.

They have created such a world emphasizing work, effort, endeavor, struggle, achievement, that they have turned almost everybody into a workaholic – which is worse than an alcoholic, because the alcoholic at least feels that he is doing something wrong. The workaholic feels he is doing the right thing, and those who are not workaholics are lazy people, worthless; they don't have any right even to exist, because they are a burden.

They have destroyed beautiful words, given them new connotations, new meanings.

For example, 'discipline'. Discipline does not mean what you have heard that it means. The word 'discipline' comes from the same root as disciple. Its root meaning is: capacity to learn, learning – to be more sensitive, to be more aware, to be more sincere, to be more authentic, to be more creative.

Life is a beautiful journey if it is a process of constant learning, exploration. Then it is excitement every moment, because every moment you are opening a new door, every moment you are coming in contact with a new mystery.

The word 'disciple' means one who learns, and 'discipline' means the process of learning.

But the word has been prostituted.

'Discipline' means obedience. They have turned the whole world into a camp of boy scouts. High above there is somebody who knows – you need not learn, you have simply to obey. They have turned the meaning of 'discipline' into its very opposite.

Learning automatically consists of doubting, of questioning, of being skeptical, of being curious – not of being a believer certainly, because a believer never learns.

But they have used the word for thousands of years in this way. And it is not only one word that they have prostituted, they have prostituted many words. Beautiful words have become so ugly in the hands of the vested interests that you cannot even imagine the original meaning of the word ... thousands of years of misuse.

They want everybody to be disciplined the way people are disciplined in the army. You are ordered – you have to do it without asking why.

This is not the way of learning.

And even from the very beginning they have imposed stories on the minds of people, that the first sin committed was disobedience. Adam and Eve were expelled from the Garden of Eden because they disobeyed.

I have tried in thousands of ways, but I don't see that they have committed any sin or any crime.

They were simply exploring. You are in a garden and you start exploring the fruits and flowers and what is edible and what is not edible.

And God is responsible, because he prohibited them from two trees—he indicated the trees: "You should not approach these two trees. One is the tree of wisdom, and the other is the tree of eternal life."

Just think, if you were Adam and Eve – was not God himself tempting you to go to these two trees? And those two trees were of wisdom and of eternal life.

Why should God be against them? If he was really a father, one who loves you, he might have pointed to them, saying that "This is a poisonous tree, don't eat from it" or, "This is the tree of death; if you eat anything, you will die."

But these two trees are perfectly right – eat as much as you can, because to be wise and to have eternal life is absolutely right.

Every father would wish his children to have wisdom and eternal life. This father seems to be absolutely loveless. Not only loveless, but as the devil said to Eve, "He has prevented you from these two trees. Do you know the reason? The reason is that if you eat from these two trees you will be equal to him, and he is jealous. He does not want you to become divine. He does not want you to become gods, full of wisdom and eternal life."

I cannot see that the devil's argument has any flaw in it. It is absolutely right. In fact, he is the first benefactor of humanity. Without him, perhaps there would have been no humanity – no Gautam Buddha, no Kabir, no Christ, no Zarathustra, no Lao Tzu ... just buffaloes, donkeys, and yankees, all eating grass, chewing grass contentedly. And God would have been very happy, that his children are very obedient.

But this obedience is poison, pure poison.

The devil must be counted as the first revolutionary of the world, and the first man to think in terms of evolution, of wisdom, of eternal life.

And God said – so the priests have been saying, the Jewish rabbis, Christian priests, Mohammedan *maulavis*, ayatollas.... They all have been saying for centuries that it was the original sin.

Again, another prostitution of a beautiful word.

The word 'sin' in its roots means forgetfulness. It has nothing to do with sin as we have come to understand it.

To forget yourself is the only sin.

And to remember yourself is the only virtue.

It has nothing to do with obedience, nothing to do with discipline.

But the people who want to exploit ... their very effort is that of a parasite, taking every drop of blood out of you. They say, "Work. Work hard, be disciplined, obey the orders – there is no need to question because the orders are coming from a higher intelligence than you have." They are in such a mind that they don't even want you to sleep.

In the Soviet Union, they are now developing a whole educational system. Every child will be educated during the day in school – but why waste his whole night? People, after a while – twenty-five years – have to come out of the university and work in the world. But they work only five hours, six hours, and their whole night is sheer wastage – it can be used. Now they are developing methods and means to use it.

For example, it can be used for teaching. The child's ears are plugged with a very subtle mechanism controlled by the central system in the town, and what they call "subliminal education" ... it does not disturb your sleep. Very slowly, so quietly that it cannot even be called whispering, because even whispering may disturb your sleep.... Its range is lower than a whisper. And the strangest thing is – which was known long before about women, but it was not known that it could be used in such a way....

About women it has been known for centuries, that if you want them to hear what you are saying, whisper. If you just start whispering with someone, any woman around is going to hear exactly what you are saying.

If you are talking loudly, nobody cares. Whispering means that you are trying to hide, something is secretive. The woman becomes alert with her more sensitive being, and she catches everything that you are saying. So if you want to say anything to any woman, just whisper it to somebody else and she will get the message absolutely correctly – and no argument!

Subliminal education is a lower range whispering. They have found that it does not disturb sleep, it does not even disturb dreams.

Dreams are here ... sleep is lower than dreams, and subliminal whispering is lower than sleep – so it simply goes underground.

For eight hours in the night you can teach continuously whatever you want to teach, and the most wonderful thing about it is that the child will remember everything – there is no need for him to memorize it, there is no need for him to do homework for it. It has simply entered into his memory system from an underground source. Now they have captured your twenty-four hours.

Even freedom to dream may be taken away one day.

It is possible that the government could decide what to dream and what not to dream. Dreams could be projected just like projecting pictures on a screen, and you would not be able to tell the difference, whether you are dreaming or the government agency is projecting some idea.

Subliminal teaching is really one of the most dangerous things discovered by the psychologists. It has been tried in many countries and found to work immensely well.

For example, you go into a movie....

You see advertisements – they work, but they need constant repetition. A certain brand of cigarette ... you have to read it in the newspaper, you have to see it on television, you have to hear it on the radio, you have to see it on the street on the billboards, you have to see it in the movie house, it has to be repeated continually. A certain brand ... you don't take any note of it. You simply read it and you forget about it, but it is going to make a mark inside you. And when you go to purchase cigarettes, suddenly you will find yourself asking for that brand.

But it is a long process.

Up to now, advertising has been a lengthy process. With subliminal teaching, it becomes very short and very dangerous.

They have tried in a few movies, experimentally, between two frames. You are watching the movie and you will not be aware that something has happened; you will go on seeing the movie. The story is going on and in just a flash – so short that you will not be able to detect with your eyes that something has passed on the screen – you feel very thirsty and you need a Coca Cola. You have not read "Coca Cola," but even though you have not read it, your memory has simply got the idea.

And they have found that on that night, in that movie house the sale of Coca Cola rose by seventy percent. The people who ask for

Coca Cola don't know *why* they are asking for Coca Cola – they feel thirsty. They are not *feeling* thirsty, they don't *need* Coca Cola, but a subliminal impact....

This is dangerous. It is taking away your freedom. You are not even free to choose, you are simply being ordered – and in such a way that you are not even aware that you have been ordered to purchase Coca Cola.

Political parties are going to use it – vote for Ronald Reagan. There is no need to destroy all the walls and write everywhere "Vote for Ronald Reagan" – just subliminal ... on television, in the movies.

And in the Soviet Union, the educationalists are thinking that everybody's night can be used for further training, refresher courses.

For example, a doctor comes out of the university.... But medical science goes on growing, and the doctor is always lagging far behind. He uses medicines which are longer   valid; science has gone farther ahead, has found better medicines. But the doctor has no opportunity to read all that literature – his night can be used.

During the day he can look at the patients; at night he can be given the latest information.

But that means you have made man a robot, twenty-four hours a day geared to work, and geared to do whatever kind of work you want. It is not his free will.

These people have brought these beautiful words like discipline, work, obedience, to such a distasteful state that it is better for a few days to abandon them completely.

Work is beautiful if it comes out of your love, if it comes out of your creativity. Then work has some spiritual quality.

Discipline is good if it comes out of your learning, your disciplehood, your dedication, your devotion – then it is something that is growing in you like a beautiful flame, directing your life in its light.

If obedience comes out of trust ... not that somebody is more powerful and if you don't listen you will be punished.

Even God could not forgive just one act of disobedience. The poor fellows ... Adam and Eve had eaten one apple!

For five years continuously I lived on apples. My mother used to say, "You should think about it – just one apple and Adam and Eve were turned out of the Garden of Eden. And you are simply *living* on apples!" For five years I didn't eat anything else.

I said, "That's what I want to see ... where? – now at the most he can drive me *into* the Garden of Eden. There are only two places, the Garden of Eden and the world. There is no other world he can drive me to."

Naturally God remained silent. "What to do now? He is committing sin from morning to night, sin upon sin" – because that was my whole food.

He could not forgive a small thing.

No, it is not the question that they had committed a great sin. The question is that God's ego is hurt; it is a revenge. With great vengeance... It is unbelievable that even now you are suffering because of the sin committed by Adam and Eve. We don't know these people – when they existed, whether they existed or not; we have no part in their act – still, we are suffering.

Every human child is going to suffer such vengeance? – it doesn't seem to be divine. God seems to be more evil than the devil. The devil seems to be more friendly, more understanding.

The people who have brought these words – work, discipline, obedience – are the priests of this God, they represent him. They have destroyed the beauty of simple words.

Obedience can also be of tremendous beauty.

But it should come out of your commitment – not out of an order from somebody.

It should come out of your heart.

You love and you respect and you are dedicated to someone so deeply that your heart always says yes; it has forgotten how to say no. Even if you want to say no, you have forgotten the word.

Then, obedience is religious, spiritual.

Beloved Osho,

In nine years of being with You, I feel that I have done all I can as far as intelligence goes to be with You. And yet now I feel in more chaos and confusion, and more ignorant than ever. I even feel on the point of giving up. Is there something I should be doing? Is there some way to be more intelligent and more wakeful? – because I am sure that I have already missed a thousand times.

It will be great if you can give up. That is the trouble. I have been telling you to give up. From the very beginning – don't start!

But you don't listen.

Nine years of great work, hard work, and still you are asking "Should I bring more intelligence and more work?"

And you think you have been missing the train because you are not working hard enough! Just the opposite is the case.

●────────────────────────── 185

You are missing the train because you are working too hard.

You are so involved in your work that you don't see that the train has come and passed. By the time you see other passengers getting out on the road ... *then* you become aware that the train has come and passed.

You simply give up and rest on the platform. So whenever the train comes.... What is the need to miss the train?

But you cannot rest, you cannot relax, you cannot let go.

You have made it a project.

You are aggressive, goal-oriented, always trying to achieve something.

And here you are with a man who is saying to you that all that you want to achieve is already within you – just relax, because only in relaxation will you realize what is hidden in you.

But you are running so fast. You don't stop, you are putting your whole intelligence ... nine years!

You could have made it the very first day you had come to me.

And you can make it right now – because the train is always standing on the platform.

It never leaves because there is nowhere to go.

Beloved Osho,

Before becoming Your sannyasin, I was desperately seeking spiritual truth. Despite what I felt to be many genuine spiritual experiences, I remained discontented and desperate.

After sannyas I began to live with Your people, work in Your communes and most of all, feel Your beauty and peace grow in my heart. In this time, my burning desires for spiritual experience and the fruits of those experiences have been slowly disappearing.

Nowadays I simply enjoy everyday life, and everything that goes with it — a tasty meal, a walk in the countryside, a good laugh with a loved one, and so on.

Beloved Master, am I getting lazy on the way to enlightenment? Can You please talk on the difference between falling asleep and letting go?

You are doing perfectly well. Just forget all about enlightenment. Enjoy simple things with total intensity.

Just a cup of tea can be a deep meditation.

If you can enjoy it, the aroma of it, slowly sipping it, the taste of it ... who cares about God?

You don't know that God is continuously feeling jealous of you when he sees you drinking a cup of tea and the poor fellow cannot have it.

Instant coffee... these things are not available in the Garden of Eden.

And since Adam and Eve left, there is no human company at all – just living with animals, who don't know how to make tea.

God is very jealous of you and very repentant that he drove Adam and Eve out of the Garden of Eden, but now nothing can be done about it. The sons and daughters of Adam and Eve are living far more beautifully, far more richly.

Enlightenment happens when you have forgotten all about it.

Don't look even out of the corner of your eye, just in case enlightenment is coming and you will miss it. Forget all about it.

You just enjoy your simple life.

And everything is so beautiful – why create unnecessary anxiety and anguish for yourself? Strange problems of spirituality.... Those things are not something you can do anything about.

If you can make your ordinary life a thing of beauty and art, all that you had always desired will start happening of its own accord.

There is a beautiful story....

There is a temple in this state, Maharashtra. It is a temple of Krishna, and a strange story is connected with the temple because the statue of Krishna – in Maharashtra he is called Bitthal – is standing on a brick. Strange, because nowhere else in any temple is any god standing on a brick.

The story is that one beautiful man, enjoying life, every bit in its totality, was so contented and so fulfilled that Krishna decided to appear before him.

Ordinarily there are people who are singing and dancing their whole life, *"Hare Krishna, Hare Rama"* and neither Rama appears nor Krishna appears – nobody appears.

This man was not bothering about Krishna or Rama or anybody. He was simply living his life, but living it in the way it should be lived with love, with heart, with beauty, with music, with poetry. His life was in itself a blessing, and Krishna has to decide that "This man needs a visit from me."

You see the story – the man is not at all thinking of Krishna – but Krishna, on his own part, feels that this man deserves a visit.

He goes in the middle of the night, not to create any trouble in the whole town. He finds the door open and he goes in.

The man's mother is very sick, and he is massaging her feet. Krishna comes behind him and says to him "I am Krishna and I have come to give you an audience, a *darshana*."

The man said, "This is not the right time; I am massaging my mother's feet."

Meanwhile, just by his side there was a brick; he pushed the brick back – he did not even look back to see who this Krishna is – he pushed the brick and told him to stand on it, and that when he is finished with his work he will see him.

But he was so much absorbed in massaging his mother's feet – because she was almost dying – that whole night passed, and Krishna remained standing there.

He said, "This is a strange stupidity. People are singing their whole life, *'Hare Krishna, Hare Rama'* and I never go there. And I have come here and this fool has not even looked back, has not even said to me, 'Sit down' but tells me to stand on the brick!"

And then it was getting light, the sun was rising, and Krishna became afraid, because people would be coming in.

The road was just by the side of the house, and the door was open – and if they saw him standing there, soon there would be trouble, great crowds would come.

So he disappeared, leaving just a stone statue of himself on the brick.

When the mother went to sleep, then the man turned and said, "Who is the fellow who was disturbing me in the night?"

And he found just a statue of Krishna.

The whole village gathered – this was a miracle, what had happened? He told the whole story.

They said, "You are a strange fellow. Krishna himself had come, and you are such a fool! You could have at least told him to sit down, offered him something to eat, something to drink. He was a guest."

The man said, "At that time there was nothing by my side except this brick. And whenever I am doing something, I do it with totality. I don't want any interference. If he is so much interested in being seen, he can come again, there is no hurry."

That statue remains in the temple of Bitthal, still standing on a brick.

But the man was really a great man – not bothering about rewards or anything, absorbed so fully in every action that the action itself becomes the reward. And even if God comes, the reward that is coming out of the totality of action is bigger than God.

Nobody has interpreted the story the way I am interpreting it, but you can see that any other interpretation is nonsense.

So just forget about spirituality, enlightenment, God – they will take care of themselves. That is their business. They are sitting there without customers.

You need not worry; you do the best you can do with life – that is your test, that is your worship, that is your religion.

And everything else will follow of its own accord.

Beloved Osho,

If the master is the one who chooses the disciple and drops him – though it may appear to the disciple that he has chosen the master, and in the course of time, has dropped him – beloved Bhagwan, why did You have to tell us?

Now I have the feeling and, fear that you might drop me at any time. Be Beloved, please don't do that to me. It hurts very much to think of it because if a man like You cannot help me, then who will? I have always been let down, and it hurts. And to think of You letting me down is too much.

Beloved Osho, please promise that You won't let me down even if I am of no use to You. I know You won't, but still that fear is there. Please be with me always, will You?

I t is a tricky question.
I can promise I will not drop you. The only problem is that if *you*

want to drop *me*, then you will find it very difficult to drop – I won't let you drop!

So now this will be your fear: I will fulfill my promise in any case – whether you want it or not!

So if this dispels your fear, perfectly good.

It is not a problem for me, I can promise.

I just don't want to interfere with anybody's freedom. I want to keep the door open; if you want to go out, I don't want to close it.

But if that is what you want, the door is closed – and locked! Now don't come next time saying that you are now fearing that if you want to get out, there is no way.

A promise is a promise!

Beloved Osho,

My beautiful master! First I wanted to run away; now I never want to leave You. What happened?

I changed my mind.

● ● ●

About Osho

Osho defies categorization, reflecting everything from the individual quest for meaning to the most urgent social and political issues facing society today. His books are not written but are transcribed from recordings of extemporaneous talks given over a period of thirty-five years. Osho has been described by the *Sunday Times* in London as one of the "1000 Makers of the 20th Century" and by *Sunday Mid-Day* in India as one of the ten people – along with Gandhi, Nehru and Buddha – who have changed the destiny of India.

Osho has a stated aim of helping to create the conditions for the birth of a new kind of human being, characterized as "Zorba the Buddha" – one whose feet are firmly on the ground, yet whose hands can touch the stars. Running like a thread through all aspects of Osho is a vision that encompasses both the timeless wisdom of the East and the highest potential of Western science and technology.

He is synonymous with a revolutionary contribution to the science of inner transformation and an approach to meditation which specifically addresses the accelerated pace of contemporary life. The unique Osho Active Meditations™ are designed to allow the release of accumulated stress in the body and mind so that it is easier to be still and in the thought-free state of meditation.

Osho International Meditation Resort

Every year the Osho International Meditation Resort welcomes thousands of people from over 100 countries who come to enjoy a holiday in an atmosphere of meditation and celebration. The 40-acre resort is located about 100 miles southeast of Mumbai (Bombay), in Pune, India, in a tree-lined residential area set against a backdrop of bamboo groves and wild jasmine, peacocks and waterfalls.

The basic approach of the resort is that of Zorba the Buddha: living in awareness, with a capacity to celebrate everything in life. Many visitors come to just be, to allow themselves the luxury of doing nothing. Others choose to participate in a wide variety of courses and sessions that support moving toward a more joyous and less stressful life by combining methods of self-understanding with awareness techniques. These courses are offered through Osho Multiversity and take place in a pyramid complex next to the famous Osho Teerth zen gardens.

You can choose to practice various meditation methods, both active and passive, from a daily schedule that begins at six o'clock in the morning. Each evening there is a meditation event that moves from dance to silent sitting, using Osho's recorded talks as an opportunity to experience inner silence without effort.

Facilities include tennis courts, a gym, sauna, Jacuzzi, a nature-shaped Olympic-sized swimming pool, classes in zen archery, tai chi, chi gong, yoga and a multitude of bodywork session. The kitchen serves international gourmet vegetarian meals, made with organically grown produce. The nightlife is alive with friends dining under the stars, with music and dancing.

Make online bookings for accommodation at the new Osho Guesthouse inside the resort through the website below or drop us an email at guesthouse@osho.com.

Take an online tour of the meditation resort, and access travel and program information at: www.osho.com/resort

BOOKS BY OSHO

EARLY DISCOURSES AND WRITINGS
A Cup of Tea
Dimensions Beyond The Known
From Sex to Superconsciousness
The Great Challenge
Hidden Mysteries
I Am The Gate
Psychology of the Esoteric
Seeds of Wisdom

MEDITATION
And Now and Here (Vol. 1 & 2)
In Search of the Miraculous (Vol. 1 & 2)
Meditation: The Art of Ecstasy
Meditation: The First and Last Freedom
Vigyan Bhairav Tantra
(boxed 2-volume set with 112 meditation cards)
Yaa-Hoo! The Mystic Rose

BUDDHA AND BUDDHIST MASTERS
The Dhammapada (Vol. 1 - 2)
The Way of the Buddha
The Diamond Sutra
The Discipline of Transcendence (Vol. 1-4)
The Heart Sutra The Book of Wisdom
(combined edition of Vol. 1 & 2)

BAUL MYSTICS
The Beloved (Vol. 1 & 2)

KABIR
The Divine Melody
Ecstasy: The Forgotten Language
The Fish in the Sea in Not Thirsty
The Great Secret
The Guest
The Path of Love
The Revolution

JESUS AND CHRISTIAN MYSTICS
Come Follow to You (Vol. 1-4)
I Say Unto You (Vol. 1 & 2)
The Mustard Seed
Theologia Mystica

JEWISH MYSTICS
The Art of Dying
The True Sage

WESTERN MYSTICS
Guida Spirituale *On the Desiderata*
The Hidden Harmony
The Fragments of Heraclitus
The Messiah (Vol. 1 & 2) *Commentaries on*

Khalil Gibran's The Prophet
The New Alchemy: To Turn You On
Commentaries on Mabel Collins'
Light on the Path
Philosophia Perennis (Vol. 1 & 2)
The Golden Verses of Pythagoras
Zarathustra: A God That Can Dance
Zarathustra: The Laughing Prophet
Commentaries on Nietzsche's
Thus Spake Zarathustra

SUFISM
Just like That
Journey to the Heart (same as Until You Die)
The Perfect Master (Vol. 1 & 2)
The Secret
Sufis: The People of the Path (Vol. 1 & 2)
Unio Mystica (Vol. 1 & 2)
The Wisdom of the Sands (Vol. 1 & 2)

TANTRA
Tantra: The Supreme Understanding
The Tantra Experience
The Royal Song of Saraha
(*same as* Tantra Vision, Vol.1)
The Tantric Transformation
The Royal Song of Saraha
(*same as* Tantra Vision, Vol.2)

THE UPANISHADS
Heartbeat of the Absolute
Ishavasya Upanishad
I Am That *Isa Upanishad*
Philosophia Ultima *Mandukya Upanishad*
The Supreme Doctrine *Kenopanishad*

Finger Pointing to the Moon
Adhyatma Upanishad
That Art Thou *Sarvasar Upanishad,*
Kaivalya Upanishad, Adhyatma
Upanishad
The Ultimate Alchemy
Atma Pooja Upanishad (Vol. 1 & 2)
Vedanta: Seven Steps to Samadhi
Akshaya Upanishad

TAO
The Empty Boat
The Secret of Secrets
Tao: The Golden Gate
Tao: The Pathless Path
Tao: The Three Treasures
When the Shoes Fits

YOGA
Yoga: The Alpha and the Omega (Vol. 1-10)

ZEN AND ZEN MASTERS
Ah, This!
Ancient Music in the Pines
And the Flowers Showered
A Bird on the Wing
(same as Roots and Wings)
Bodhidharma: The Greatest Zen Master
Communism and Zen Fire, Zen Wind
Dang Dang Doko Dang
The First Principle
God is Dead: Now Zen is the only Living Truth